The Sacred Everyday

A Search for the Exquisite Beauty of an Ordinary Life

By Mackenzie Chester

© 2023 by Mackenzie Chester
Published by Early Wren Press

Book design and images by Mackenzie Chester

Visit Mackenzie's blog, The Sacred Everyday, at
www.mackenziechester.com

I dedicate this book to my mother and father and eight siblings, who gave me the gift of childhood. And to my husband and eight children, who gave me the gift of motherhood.

Table of Contents

Introduction

A Few Words About This Book

Voices of My Life

14 Voices of My Life, An Abridged Biography

18 Brave (Names Strangers Call Me in the Grocery Store)

26 Questions to My Future Self

32 Sometimes I Travel Through Time

35 The Girl in This Photograph (Me by the Sea, 1985)

37 My One Small Voice

40 Other People's Houses

43 There Is a Woman in the Mirror

46 The Climax of a Real Story

Slow Work

50 Motherhood Begins With Surrender

62 Slow Work

57 This Morning I Sat Down With My 22-Year Old Self

63 In Time

66 For Which My Heart Is Yearning

68 Listening for the Song

72 Surrendering to a Season

76 My Daughter Plays the Piano

77 The Sacred Everyday

STANDING IN THE HALLWAY OF SORROW

82   Miss and Carry

87   Standing in the Hallway of Sorrow

91   Being There (On the Shores of Life and Loss)

96   My Beautiful Dying Mother, A Birth Story

101 First Birthday (Love Song for a Baby)

104 Grief is a River

107 Broken Open-Hearted Love

109 Grief and the Path of Beauty

114 The Memory of an Unexpected Rain

EVERY MORNING I WAKE IN AN OCEAN

118 Every Morning I Wake in an Ocean

120 Bridge to Peace

123 The Story of Yesterday

127 Every Choice Is Too Hard

134 Embracing This Breath

137 This Morning I Was Born

140 I Stand in This Breath of My Life

142 Hope On the Inhale

Questions at 2 a.m.

148 The Space Between Here and a Miracle

153 On Words (In Every Storm, Mercy)

156 Looking Deeply Inside Myself

159 The Sleeping Face of My Beautiful Boy

161 Living With Vision

165 Keeping Part of You Alive

169 Poem at 2 a.m.

Faith and Miracles

172 Are You Going to Have More?

178 Helpless (When Faith Trembles)

182 My Heart Trembles and Sings

183 How Do You Feed Them?

194 Memory and Promise of Light

196 The Dreams of a Stranger (The Story of a Miracle)

One Small Garden

212 Tending the Life I Am Given

215 Vision and Hindsight, A Tale of Two Lists

220 Beauty in the Midst of Darkness

223 The Woman and the Seed (A Parable)

233 Acknowledgements

Introduction

My mama had nine children. I am the youngest. The fact that I even exist in this world is not a small miracle. I see it now, like the iconic scene in It's a Wonderful Life, where Mary is closing up the library. *A world where I don't exist.* My husband is scorching himself a grilled cheese with curry powder and jalapeños in his lonely house in the middle of nowhere, listening to a podcast, just home from who knows what kind of work. There are no children around his table. None of the soft, sweet smiles that only the faces of his babies can bring out in his eyes.

Our children, unrealized dreams. Their faces, unpainted portraits. Their voices, songs unsung.

But the miracle happened.

I was born.

For this three-word sentence, I will always be grateful to my dear, sweet, selfless mother who opened herself up for me to travel to this world. From these words flash the infinite scenes—one after the other—of an entire life-story. All of the colors of sunrise and sunset, the sharp sweetness of violinsong and piano, the ache and longing and hope of a beating heart. The smell of rain and honeysuckle, the touch of two hands, the spark of eyes meeting, the taste of fresh bread and strong tea, the mind's library of memory and experience. All the wonder and mystery flows forth from the beautiful terrible moment: birth. I will never get over the miraculous gift of an ordinary life.

This book is an invitation into my lifelong search to find God in every single moment, from the most mundane to the most extraordinary. I have searched for him in every tense—looking backwards and forwards and trying to linger longer in each experience to find Him in the present. I have looked for him on the pages of journals, at the bottom of the laundry pile, in the ocean waves of sadness, in the hollow ache of grief, in the bright golden glow of morning light, in the songs of birds and the words of friends.

I hope that these pages will illuminate the love and beauty of our God, who is teaching me, day by day, that miracles abound in the details of our wonderful, ordinary lives. They are there, waiting for us to have eyes that see, ears that hear, and hearts that understand the beautiful truth that He is with us. That life—every single day of it—is a sacred gift.

A Few Words About This Book

This book is a collection of thoughts, writing, blog posts, and journal entries that span the last decade of my life. I have arranged the entries much like a book of poetry is put together—by theme and not by chronology. (It is for this reason that my age and number of children in each story seems to fluctuate.) There are some passages that I have brought up-to-date, combining my first thoughts with current ones. I have also altered some passages for brevity's sake or for clarification purposes, but for the most part, I have presented the stories in their original format. I have included dates when the passage has been largely unaltered from its first version on my blog or in my journals, especially when it reflects a specific season of my life.

This book is more like a diary or journal than anything else. It represents a decade of trying to find God in the ordinary details of beautiful, exhausting motherhood, of relearning who I am, finding my way through grief, and pressing in to find hope in a dark world. I offer this book to you as a friend with more questions than answers, with sincere hope that it encourages you as you are making your way through your own sacred everyday life.

The book can be read in one sitting or it can be taken in any order. Each entry is a stand-alone piece. Feel free to start wherever the words grab at you.

A few details about who I am may be helpful in case you are going to close your eyes and put your finger on a random page to begin. So let me tell you a bit about myself.

I am married to Randy Chester, a mad-scientist musician. We have eight children ages 20 months, 3, 6, 8, 9, 11, 13, and 15. From our home, we record music and I write, design, and record The Sacred Everyday Blog and Podcast. If you were to stop by our house unannounced, you would see stacks of books, witness enormous creative messes, and hear music showcasing varying degrees of accomplishment. You would no doubt hear laughing, crying, singing, and yelling. You would see dishes and laundry, probably piled high. Depending on the day, I might be fully immersed in the beauty of it or I might be wrestling with my desire to run to a quiet room, lock the door, and try to make sense of the life God has given me.

I aspire to remember that every moment of my life has meaning. I long to find peace in the chaos of a houseful of creative, curious souls. I desperately want to press into the beauty of the life I have been given. More than anything, I want my life to bring glory to God. In him I live and breathe and have my being.

This is my life and story. Welcome. Make yourself at home.

VOICES OF MY LIFE

VOICES OF MY LIFE,
AN ABRIDGED BIOGRAPHY

It's easy to look back over years as a series of big events—the day I was born, schools I attended, graduations, marriage, jobs held, the birthdays of my children. . . These are the visible rings around my tree, the important details in a brief biography of my life.

But when I close my eyes and let my thoughts steep like a good, strong cup of early morning tea, I hear a thousand voices whispering past conversations. Words. Music. Beginning with the sweet, angelic voice of my beautiful mother. I see her in my memory, watching over me as a child. I hear her singing by moonlight, calming my fears. Planting seeds in my heart of what it means to lay down your life as a living sacrifice. I stumbled my way through the dark forest of my bedroom every night of my childhood to make it to the safe castle of her song.

I remember the rich, coffee-colored voice of my father. His laughter. The honest, quick step. How it felt to be a girl, to sit beside him on the couch and watch a movie late at night until I could no longer fight sleep and didn't want to anyway. And that incredible moment of surrender and falling. . .

How many mornings did I find myself tucked snugly in my warm bed with no memory of his strong arms lifting and carrying me up the stairs, laying me gently down, arranging my blankets, and blessing me with his gently-spoken prayer of goodnight.

I hear the voices of my brothers and sisters. Fighting, laughing, crying, whispering, singing, yelling. "Here I come, ready or not!" I hear our footsteps running circles through the house, wearing grooves into the floor.

The sound of my first guitar, strummed in the church parking lot—a gift from my oldest sister for no special occasion. The songs we used to sing, sitting around the living room. Mama at the piano, Daddy whistling as he walked through the house with a handful of freshly cut flowers from the garden.

I remember the music of my sisters' voices—all of them, on walks around the block, or to the rhythm of wheels on pavement as we drove back and forth to school and church. I remember sitting on my sister's bed and watching her draw. The patient way she showed me how to make arms with hands and fingers. I remember conversations in dark cars with my brothers on the way home from prayer meetings and movie theaters. I remember my sister's face in the dark where we shared a room. I remember the day she left for college. I remember how I sobbed like a baby the day I sang at her wedding.

I am struck by the memory of the incomparable voice of my husband-to-be. The day I was driving to school, listening to him sing on my car stereo, and love hit me like a car crash.

There were all the people who hung out in the art building. Professors, friends, the words of writers and poets, the sound of music. Then there were friends who were in love, friends who were married, friends with children, friends who bake bread, friends who write. . . There were all those late-night conversations standing in parking lots, sitting over potlucks, hanging out after shows, driving on highways, sharing pots of tea.

And scores could be written from the musical voices of children. I am continually changed by their song that is moving through me.

Looking back over my life, I am amazed at how we have found our way here. *There were so many people.* They stand in my memory like illuminated shadows. I remember their words. The threads of living conversation that have woven themselves into the very fabric of the life we are now wearing as a garment. People who spoke life into my soul. People who unknowingly changed my life by telling me stories about their own. People who showed me truth by walking and breathing and letting life move through them like a song. Who gave me hope that marriage can be better than worse. Who showed me that children are a blessing, not a curse. Who gave me courage to seek a life of vision for myself and my family.

I stand on these words. I sleep under them like a blanket. I build my house on them. I drink them down in cups of tea. I speak them. I write them. On nights like these, I wrap myself up in them and cry like a baby.

Life is such a gift. There were so many people. And there are so many people. And the intersection of our lives, our words, our worlds. . .

These are the details that make our stories worth telling.

BRAVE

(NAMES STRANGERS CALL ME IN THE GROCERY STORE)

Sometimes people don't know what to say.

When they see us in the grocery store—three little ones in the buggy, three bigger ones swarming around my waist, two walking beside me—I can actually see them doing math in their heads. Is it possible that all of these children could belong to the same mother?

I get a lot of looks and comments.

"You have your hands full."

"Are they all yours?"

"You know how this happens, don't you?"

(There are just so many brilliant ways to answer this question. But I usually just smile, nod, and keep them to myself.)

"Wow, you are really brave."

I like this one. Because it is actually a meaningful reminder to me of the work God is doing in my life through having and raising children.

When people look at me with my eight kids in the grocery store, and they say I'm brave, I think a few of them really mean it. But I suspect most mean that by having all of these children, I am making my life exponentially more difficult than it needs to be. That life is hard enough already. I must be "brave" to bring all of these children into the world and all this responsibility onto myself.

But the truth is this: I *am* brave.

And do you know what God has used in my life to make me brave?

Having children.

I'll tell you what I mean.

When we decided we were ready to let things happen and open ourselves up to being parents, let's face it: we were clueless. There was a certain bravery involved. Stepping out into the unknown. But most of us follow this path—grow up, marry, and have children. So it didn't require a lot of initial courage or bravery. It was what we all expected to happen.

But as soon as our first child was thrust into this world and we locked eyes on her and realized she would be depending on us to keep her alive, a seed of true bravery began to grow. Those early months of her life, I was shocked and awed by the reality that I had never before understood: My life is not my own. My body is not my own. My mind is not even my own. Between waking and sleeping, middle-of-the-night feedings, healing, processing, anticipating and meeting the constant needs, I began to feel lost in my own life. But when I saw that dear little face, I knew that somehow I would have to learn to find my way. I had to live. And I had to live as true a life as possible. Because this little baby was in my care.

This is when I first began to be brave.

Birth traumatized me. I was walking around with eyes opened to the obvious, yet bleak reality that this is the only way that children are born into this world. I remember thinking that birth was like a monster that came out of my body and turned me inside out and tried to kill me. Then when it was over, he went back to sleep. In the first months after our baby's birth, I used to cry because I knew we wanted our baby to one day have a brother or sister. I was terrified. I was filled with the dread of walking that road again. I didn't want to meet the monster a second time.

But slowly and surely, the seed of courage began to grow.

God was merciful to me. We were surprised to find ourselves expecting again when our first child was 10 months old. I had nine months to process, to pray, to journal, to grow in my faith and courage. Our second daughter was born, and when she moved through my body and into our arms, I felt a fog physically lift from my mind. I can only describe it as this: her birth healed me.

And I became a little more brave.

Every birth has changed my life and required a commitment to be braver than I wanted to be. Each birth has challenged my faith in God and brought me deeper into communion with Him. Having children causes us to have courage we can only fathom after we have been called upon to use it.

The lady ringing up my groceries told me that she would never bring children into this world. She told me that watching the news had convinced her that life wasn't going to get any better. I understand.

When you have children, everything horrible in this world becomes more horrible. All the evils in the world, even briefly imagined upon the perfect, trusting face of a little child, is enough to make me want to run away, screaming. All of the accidents, the diseases, wars and rumors of wars, the people who care nothing for the sacredness of human life. . . And not just any human life—but this—my precious, helpless, indescribably beautiful, hopeful, trusting, achingly sweet and loving child. Sharing life with these little ones opens us up to the possibility of all kinds of pain, real and imagined. They remind us how raw love is. How much it can hurt. How deep it goes.

I'm not going to lie. There are times I want to shield myself from the severity and depth of this kind of love. I didn't know living required so much courage until I had little ones. The world seems bleaker and darker than ever when I think of them standing in it.

But at the same time, when you have children, everything beautiful in this world becomes more beautiful. The moon, a cup of tea, the sharp, sweet surprise of honeysuckle after rain. Fireflies, dark chocolate, the indescribable perfection of a seashell. . . Sharing life with children opens us back up to wonder. They remind us that life is a gift. And the world seems so much richer, so much more full of light and life when I think of them standing in it.

Children know secrets that we have all forgotten. They forgive easily and completely. They know how to love deeply, without question and without fear. They know how to enjoy the little things in life. How to live in the moment. How to embrace change. How to bask in the beauty of an ordinary day.

When life is bleak, children draw us out of our winter. When we are grieving, children surround us with love and comfort and remind us to see beauty.

And when we would shut ourselves up for fear of all the heartache in this world, they call us to take courage. To love deeper and wider and higher than the walls that we have built around our lives to protect ourselves from pain.

Yes, I am.

Brave.

And every beautiful soul that has passed through this body has made me braver. Through childbirth, I have learned to lean into the comforting truth that my life is not my own. And that it never was. And I am learning that I don't have to struggle against this. All I have to do is live, trust God, and take one breath at a time. I do not have to carry all of the fears of the future. I am not in control. And I never was. Thank God. And God will bring me (and these children) through this life, breath by breath, and deliver us.

I know that in this life, I will most likely be called upon to summon courage that I cannot now even begin to comprehend. But I do have a confident hope that God will see me through. He has started a good work in me, and He will finish it to completion. I know that God will walk with me. I know that Christ, who laid down His life for me, will continue to teach me to lay my life down for these children. That He will help me to trust their lives into His hands. That He will help me to lay down my fears and gather up my courage. I know that God has used these little ones to draw me out of my own self and my own fears and to make me brave.

And so I am grateful for the many reminders of the work of Christ in my life.

"Wow, you are really brave to bring eight kids into this world."

Yes, I am. Because God is with me. And He is using these children to bring so much beauty and joy and light and life to this earth.

And day by day, little by little, season by season, they are making me brave.

QUESTIONS TO MY FUTURE SELF
OCTOBER 27, 2020

This morning I am checking in with my future self. I have to
gently wake her, because it is 4:30 a.m., and she is no longer
in the habit of waking with babies all through the night. When
she sees me standing there over her bed in the dark, she
doesn't mind. She treats me as she would her own child,
quietly getting up and following me to the kitchen table.

I have a pot of tea waiting. We take a sip of Darjeeling and set
down our cups in perfect synchronization. She looks at me.
She asks me what is on my mind.

I just hope I am doing this right, I say, half-embarrassed, even
though it is me I am speaking to.

I half-hope she is going to tell me how it all turns out. How
we navigated our way through the second decade of
parenting, how homeschooling had indeed been the right
route for our family, and how God had led us every step of the
way. I want her to tell me that my children, who are sleeping
in their beds at ages 12, 11, 9, 7, 5, 3, and 18 months are
enjoying their future lives. That they love learning. That they
love each other. That they love God. That they are living out
the purposes for which they were each individually, uniquely

26

created. I want her to tell me that we have beautiful, meaningful conversations with them at ages 22, 21, 19, 17, 15, 13, and 10. And that we have a bond that will never be broken.

I want her to tell me that this vision that I carry in my heart for my children is attainable, even though they have parents who are imperfect. In spite of the great chasm between my wonderful, inspired intentions and the reality of our busy, needs-never-stop life. I want to know that we are moving in the right direction. Did they learn all they needed to know for their lives? Are they still learning and growing? Is it going to turn out ok?

I take a breath, and dare to look into her eyes.

She doesn't speak. We both know she can't answer my questions. We have agreed more than once that it is best not to know too much about our own future. Instead, she eyes my green bag, casually draped across the table. She reaches inside and pulls out my journal. *May I?* she asks.

Of course, I respond. She flips through the pages. I watch her face light up with long-forgotten memories.

This was a big year for you, she mused. *Your year of creative fire. You showed your daughters how to be a mother and still* connect deeply with your creative voice. You allowed them to serve you. I remember how hard that was for you, but how naturally they took on many of the responsibilities of your home for that season. Such a seed planted for their future, she said.

This was the year the bakery opened, wasn't it? And you started taking the kids in pairs to spend the morning there? Oh, I loved those mornings when they were still so young. Eating cinnamon rolls, painting with watercolors and folding origami in the back corner of the cafe. Talking about anything and everything. They were so delighted to be there with you. Do you remember?

She continued to turn the pages. She stopped on August 26 of this year and sighed. Her eyes lingered over the words I had scrawled across the page in tear-soaked ink. *This is the year we lost Mama. I remember how raw the ache felt then. I remember how your children gathered around you. How they learned to comfort you. I am so glad they were home with you. You showed them how to pass through the waters of grief with grace. And they showed you how to get out of bed when the sorrow was heavy like a weighted blanket. They woke you up each morning to joy and beauty.*

I nodded my head, wiping my eyes. She turned the page and suddenly laughed through tears. *You are going to have another baby! Oh, Mackenzie. If you only knew how much this child is going to be adored by all of you. How much all of your children will learn from this little one. Right now I know it seems surreal. But let me assure you, this child has a name and a future and without question belongs in your family. I have seen this baby's beautiful face.* Here she paused and laughed again. *Your life will never be the same. And over the years to come, you will fall down on your knees over and over again, thanking God for his mercy in giving you this precious child.*

By now I am sobbing. She is still turning my pages.

She stops on a prayer I scribbled down, asking God for vision, for wisdom, to guide me, to help me to teach my children the things they needed to know this day. Praying over their lives, their futures. That God would provide everything they need, that he would put the people and experiences in their paths that would shape them into the people he created them to be.

She pauses and lifts her gaze up to meet mine.

What is it? I ask.

She tells me that she, herself, has written an identical prayer just this week. *I don't have all the answers,* she says. *I am still praying over the lives of these children. The story is far from over. I am still walking in faith, still praying that God will do all of these things, answer all of these promises, that our children will not only be okay in such an uncertain world, but that they will be living lives that are beautiful and inspiring and leading others to the hope of Christ. Everything is not going to be easy. But there is joy and beauty in every season if you choose to search for it. There will be many more days ahead when you feel unqualified for the great responsibility of raising these precious souls. But God will use every detail of your life that you offer up to him. You can't always see it now, but He is guiding you. He hears your prayers, and He is leading your family down the best pathway for your lives. These prayers are changing the course of your children's futures. More than anything you teach them at the table. More than any book or curriculum. Never stop praying like this. God hears and honors these prayers. Do you trust him?*

Do you trust him?

These words resonate in my soul. She knows it. She flips to the next blank page of my journal and nudges it toward me. She waits. I pick up my pen and write today's date. In slow, careful letters, I write the question on paper: do you trust him? And with each stroke, I imprint these words on my heart to carry me through the next season of raising these beautiful, precious, unique-in-all-the-world souls. I put down my pen and close my journal.

She smiles, stands, and says she needs to go before people start waking up for breakfast. I agree, give her a quick hug, and say goodbye.

I sit for a few more moments in the quiet, early-morning kitchen. I finish my pot of tea to a small chorus of back-deck birdsong, watching the sun rise on a new day. In the scattered golden and pink light of mercies, new every morning, I let my fears for the future go. I send them away on the wings of a little sparrow, who flies off into the distance and out of my sight.

And I make my choice.

Today, I will trust Him.

SOMETIMES I TRAVEL THROUGH TIME

Sometimes I travel through time. Usually in the middle of the night, when I am awake with babies on either side of me, not daring to move lest I wake them and lose the few precious moments I have to let my thoughts flow without interruption. During the days, the needs take over, and I don't have time to be anywhere but here, moment by moment, wrestling with all of the daily tasks of raising a family and making a living and trying to do the best I can at existing on earth in this human body.

But in the middle of the night, I go to the past. To my childhood, where I was a girl who was waking from a nightmare. My eyes opened in the dark and I climbed out of my bed and stumbled my way, crying, to the bed of my mother and father. They woke easily. My mother sang to me. She told me that I could only think about one thing at a time, and if I was scared, I should try to think about happy things. I took blankets from the closet, made myself a soft pallet on their floor, and went back to sleep, dreaming of my next birthday.

Sometimes, when the house is dark and quiet and all the little ones are sleeping and still, I go to the future. To the many-possible-endings of the history that is now being written for us. I think about my children, who may wake from nightmares that are all too real. I think about everything I read on social media today, and I apply that to the future. And my gut reaction is fear.

It's going to be okay.

These words form in my mind, and I am not sure if they are from the voice of my mother in the past or my own voice in the future, or if they are breathed by the Holy Spirit himself.

But I listen.

It is so easy to get lost in the ifs of life. **What if** this happens. . . Or, **if only** things could have been different. . .

But even in the longest run-on sentence of chaos, pain, sickness, death, disaster, war, violence, and bleak uncertainty, we cannot quake beneath the quivering question mark. We cannot be pinned down, paralyzed by a two-letter word. We belong to a kingdom that is eternal and sure, not wavering, not set in the tension of the present moment. We look for God in every tense of our lives, and when we search with all our hearts, we will find Him. He has never left us. He has never forsaken us. He never will.

THE GIRL IN THIS PHOTOGRAPH
(ME BY THE SEA, 1985)

When you were a child, did you lose yourself at the seashore and forget life aches? Did you run to the waters laughing?

I go back to the ocean of my childhood, where I was the girl in this photograph. My mother, on the other side of the camera, has eyes that sparkle blue and deep and a face that smiles my name. I cannot separate my own love for the ocean from my mother's love for me and her love of the sea. In my memory, she is there, bare feet in the sand, hair as bright as sunshine that moves in slow-motion to the sound of unaccompanied cello. She has a body and a voice I can hear. She has not yet flown to some distant shore, familiar but unreachable, like the song you knew as a child but forgot how to sing.

I want the waves to whisper something, but they are still. Suspended in time, they do not roar, they do not call me. They are sketched with silver upon paper and will never swell or break again. These are the facts of the photograph. They are held by laws of light that only memory and imagination may transcend.

Hope is the whole motion of the ocean, but grief comes in waves and lasts till it passes. It sharpens photographs and

35

softens memory, etching the image of a future where lives do not end but go on eternal—as far as the eye can see and beyond the horizon of calm sea.

I think of all the things I should say to the child in this photograph to prepare her for the moment when she will be a woman writing a poem about the death of her mother.

I search her face. I smile her name. And all I can say is this: enjoy your day at the beach.

But she is laughing and singing and running to the shore, and she does not hear.

MY ONE SMALL VOICE

Standing at the edge of still waters
in the middle of my life
looking out on the reflection of the world that God in his
lovingkindness
created for me
to inhabit
and enjoy

The beauty of trees, sky, grass
the V-line of geese mirrored above
and before me
the sound of wind
the distant moving rush of river
the hum of every living thing
and the one small voice
of my life

All the people who held me up
from my childhood forward
gave me laughter, love, song
a heart that was unafraid
to love and be loved,
I see them now reflected,
rippling out into the distance

37

It takes so many lives
to shape one life
So many hands
to build one story.

O God of grace,
for the indescribable riches of your love,
I have only the one small song
of my singular life
to sing in return

Every moment you work miracles—
the breath in my lungs
the kindness of strangers
the eye that sees
the hope that rises
above all fear
the light that shines
in the darkest night

For all these treasures
you ask nothing more
than the story of my life.

It is not enough.

But I give it back
with my whole heart
body, mind, soul and strength.

Poet, God
My great hope:
To have your handwriting
Scrawled upon the pages of my life.
To be lyrics of a song
Never before sung

My one small voice
is all I have to give.

OTHER PEOPLE'S HOUSES
OCTOBER 18, 2020

My daughters and I pulled in at Michelle's house before she arrived. We knew we were welcome to go on in. By the time I wrangled with my couple of bags, the girls had already run inside. I entered the front door, set down my things, and walked into the kitchen. This is what I saw: Rosie and Paloma with their favorite borrowed mugs in hand, standing in the kitchen, making cups of tea. Paloma was dressed in a Red-Ridinghood cape. Rosie was barefoot. They were completely themselves, relaxed, welcomed, loved, and they felt probably more at-home in this moment than they did when we left our own house.

Michelle arrived, delighted we had already started the tea. We sat at the little round table, and she brought out a plate of cookies she had made for us. We began to talk. The kind of talk that breathes new life into all of us. I watched my girls settle into a slow pace and the sweet peace of knowing that we were going to be here for two glorious hours, that no one would need us to grab a baby or wipe a spill. There would be no reasoning with two-year-olds, no intercepting minor disasters, no interruptions, no unexpected change of plans. We were here. At the table. In a friend's home. We made it to a safe place where we could sit and just *be*.

At my friend's table, my girls came alive. I realized how they are growing. How much they have to say. How deeply they feel. How easily they share. In someone else's house, I gave them my full attention, as I would to any other dear friend who shared a cup of tea with me. I felt a glow of gratitude that we were able to experience this sweet time together.

What an incredible gift it is to enter the house of a friend who has no other purpose than to love and listen to and bless you.

I want my house to be this for others. But I also want it to be this *for my own children*. Why is it such a struggle to slow down long enough to have a long, slow conversation with them at my own table? My husband and children are the dearest people to me in this life. How can I learn the art of welcoming them to this table? Of slowing down, of having conversations that are paced and easy and meander where they will. Why is this so much easier at other people's houses?

If I'm honest, I am sometimes so focused on checking one more meal off the day's to-do list that I miss the heart of what is happening at this table. The beauty of these little souls, gathered around in a sacred circle. Our eyes meeting, our bodies nourished, our souls connecting, our spirits lifting up thanks to God for his provision. This is where we share life.

I want to slow down and see the beauty in it. I want to listen to my children as if I were listening to an intimate friend. I want to sit at the table. To linger there. To love deeply. To allow my children to breathe a sigh of relief because we made it to a safe place where we can just sit and *be*. To show them that one of the greatest joys of my life is to welcome them, to hear them, to love them, to bless them, and to simply *be* with them. To see them here as I see them at other people's houses.

THERE IS A WOMAN IN THE MIRROR

There is a woman in the mirror that shares my face but does not know who I am. She mimics my every move with nuanced attention to detail—the slight raise of brow, the synchronized blink and focus, the parting lips and hint of smile. . . Her performance is flawless. But she doesn't know what I am thinking.

She follows with her eyes as I move through the motions of my life. She sees me in passing intervals, in mirrored images. In 15-second clips or live photos as I walk by.

She imagines herself cast as the lead role in a comedy of errors. The perpetual rerun of a meaningless day. She sees me with armfulls of babies. She pantomimes my wrestling them into clothes and habits and sitting them down at the kitchen table. She watches the time-lapse movie of endless spills and meals and messes.

She sees me bent over a manuscript in the early morning hours, scratching away at the story of my life.

She sees me touching the faces of my children, speaking to them, leaning over their drawings, listening to their songs.

She sees me breaking up fights and absolutely throwing my hands up in the air.

She smiles when I smile. She cries when I cry.

She is bystanding my life. From inside the frame, she watches me half-heartedly, like a boring mini-series, wondering when we will ever get to the climax of the story. She is only invested because we share this face.

But she doesn't know my secrets.

She doesn't know the words that are building a city in my mind. That I move through a life where the streets are lit by the phrases of poets and writers. Where houses are framed in the sturdy conversations of kindred friends. Where the sprawling streets are called by the names of those I love most dearly. I live in a city built upon the profound comfort and calm of holy scripture, the musical voices of children, the language that lingers in the places we gather, the heart-beating bleeding of ink on paper. I live in hymned harmonies and hopes sung. I build my house on words. I rest my restless heart in them.

She could not know that every moment is moving me forward into the story of God's great love. That He can be found in the smallest of days. That significance can be secret, like a seed planted in the ground.

Like the smile we share as I walk on by.

THE CLIMAX OF A REAL STORY

The climax of a real story is always moving: growing up, graduation, true love, marriage, becoming a mother, getting the kids to bed so you can finally sit down for the evening, hitting send to the publisher after a decade of writing, getting the kitchen clean after breakfast.

In stories, there is one climax. And then there is the hope of sustained joy. There isn't time for the mini-dramas of the everyday. There is only time for the two-hour special, the one big problem, overcome, against all odds, where love comes shining through and saves the day.

But this moment is the climax of your story. Whether you are sitting in grief or surrounded by those you hold dear. *Because you are alive.* And your body is activated by the sacred breath of beautiful life, spirit housed by flesh and bone. You are not a lifeless body, but body, soul and spirit moving as one.

This is the moment that touch can be reciprocated. That words are not just ink and memory, but flow forth as voice and song from the living human soul.

The day is yours. This moment, a gift. There is no time for fear or regret.

If you want to understand your life you must recognize this: this moving moment is the most important moment of your unfinished story.

So take a deep breath, be brave, and live.

SLOW WORK

MOTHERHOOD BEGINS WITH SURRENDER

Motherhood begins with surrender.
For the sake of love, yes,
but surrender all the same.
The body the mind the soul the spirit
bends to the body that breaks open
the womb, the silent seed
that buries itself into the earth
of the secret place within.

If birth isn't surrender
forget everything I've ever said.
Or don't you remember when all you could do
was stay alive while the waves
broke over your body
to bring this baby to the shore
of a new world

Motherhood is the surrender of plans
of dreams of hopes great and small
of sleep and a certain kind of freedom
To go where you want
when you want, how you want
to hold a picture in your mind
of who you truly are

It is adding another set of desires
to your own desires.
It is calling up a radiant hope for another life.
It is seeing a life flashing before your eyes
that is not your own life
and knowing that no matter how
hard you try to do everything right
this child will walk in a broken world

And you still have to learn
to surrender him back up to God
day by breaking day, night by waking night

And this surrender is holy, sweet, and sacred
because it is for the sake of love.

SLOW WORK

NOVEMBER 24, 2015

God is doing a slow work in me. So many days it feels like nothing is happening. Like my life, which once seemed so useful and productive, is making zero impact on the world. The days when my identity was defined by an impressive string of accomplishments are lost somewhere at the bottom of the laundry pile. There are moments when the words "three meals a day" can strike a chord of terror in my heart. I can actually see them: hundreds of thousands of meals that I will be responsible for, stretching out into eternity.

Sometimes it feels like all I do is fail miserably at trying to maintain a messy house. Like the crowning achievement of my life would be to mop the kitchen floor.

I want more than this.

I remember when people used to ask me what I do. "I am a musician." "I'm an artist." "I'm a teacher." "I'm a writer." My identity was so much clearer then. Now, I don't even know how to answer.

"I'm mostly a Mommy."

What does that even mean?

Life with five small children is beautiful and messy and, of course, exhausting. I chose this life. I want this life. I love this life. I know it is passing by right before my eyes and that one day I will mourn the loss of it.

God is doing a slow work in me.

Motherhood is changing me so much that I sometimes hardly recognize myself. Sometimes it feels like I am not accomplishing anything that is tied to the identity I once considered to be my true self. Children work on you like erosion on the soil, loosening everything that will come up, leaving only what is solid beneath. The me that I imagined is mostly worn away. I am still wrestling with the fact that my life is not my own, even though I should have known this all along.

God is doing a slow work in me.

Marriage is changing me. Sometimes marriage can be like the effects of weather and natural disasters on the earth of your heart. Can the ground stay fertile? Will we continue to do the hard labor of moving out debris from every devastating earthquake and rebuild? Will we anchor our hearts together through the storms? God, this work is hard. It takes a willingness to live in a constant state of forgiveness—giving it, asking for it, and receiving it. But there is enough sunlight and rain for beautiful things to grow here. God, please let this love grow.

God is doing a slow work in me.

I have a suspicion that this is what we are really aiming for in marriage and in raising children. Slow work. It is not about how much we accomplished today. It is about what is happening deep in the core of our beings, the slow work that God is doing in our hearts. It is living in collaboration with one another, surrendering to the clear will of God to offer up our whole selves as living sacrifices. Up to this point in my life, God has given me no clearer opportunity to do this than to be a wife and mother. The life I have now is one that I never imagined. I am a changed woman. My identity is so much fuller and complex. My soul is knit together with the man that I love. We are one person. Everything he does is part of me. Each child that has moved through my body has changed me deeply, from the inside out. As my children grow and change, so they grow and change me. Their emotions deepen my own. When they grieve, my heart aches in a new place. Their joy fills me fuller. The baby touches all of our lives. We share her and grow more loving because of her.

God is doing a slow work in me.

One day I may have a whole day to myself again. To write songs or make art. To learn to sew. To write that book that I really want to get out of me. In the meantime, I have to lay aside my old ideas of what being productive looks like. I can only do what I can find time to do. But even now, I remind myself to look at what is happening: every day, my house is full of artwork and laughter and music. My four year old son illustrates stacks of stapled-together-paper books every day. My daughters create paper dolls and play the Irish whistle. My two year old designs cities out of wooden blocks. The baby is inventing her very own dear little version of sign language. So much of the mess of this house is because they are making beautiful things. They are beginning their creative mark on the world. Their work is inspired and prolific. And I feel that in some way, it is an extension of the beauty that I myself wanted to add to this world. They are doing it for me, better than I could do it myself, in their own voices and with their own hands. And this is just the beginning of the beauty their lives will bring.

God is doing a slow work in me.

And I want to surrender to that work. To press into it. To find meaning in the barely perceptible changes. I want to see every endless pile of laundry as part of this work. To see each meal as a blessing. To walk through every season with thankfulness, not clinging to the old idea of who I am, but allowing God to work in me in his time and his way. I want to walk in step with the Spirit, and allow him to make me the woman it will take a long, slow lifetime to become.

THIS MORNING I SAT DOWN WITH MY 22-YEAR-OLD SELF

This morning I sat down at the table with my 22-year old self. She drank ginger peach black tea with cream and sugar. I drank darjeeling, black. We met in a cafe, the kind with classical music and the pleasant hum of conversation in the background. We both had open journals on the table and laughed about how we shared the same favorite pen. The people sitting next to us wondered if we were sisters or if I was the mother and she was the daughter. It was clear we were related, but there were definitely significant years between us.

We met by chance earlier this year and had been planning this breakfast date for months, but both of our schedules have been so busy we couldn't meet until now. We didn't know we were the same person.

I asked her how life was. She prattled on about grad school and her first year of marriage. She showed me a stack of photographs that she had made in the darkroom. She is going to school, making art, and trying to start a photography business to help pay bills. She and her husband are just starting out—they are clearly deeply in love and finding their way through the first small struggles of building a life together. It is moving to see someone so freshly in love. It stirs up a bittersweet longing in me to experience those days again.

She asks me what my life is like. I tell her that I have eight children, that we homeschool, that we teach music lessons from our home. I told her that we get to eat every meal together as a family, and that I consider it one of God's greatest kindnesses to me that my husband and I both work from home and get to raise our children together. She laments how little she gets to see her husband. Between her schooling, teaching, and his 10-7 job, they are starved for time together. I remember days like that, I tell her. It's tough. She asks me what it is like to be married for nineteen years. I am completely honest with her. I tell her it is wonderful.

She tells me that she hates it when people tell her to wait till the honeymoon is over. I roll my eyes and laugh and agree. I tell her that people never stop saying things like that. When you have children, it's: wait until he's walking, wait until she hits the terrible twos, wait until they're teenagers. . . I tell her I don't believe in those kinds of statements anymore. I tell her that love grows and deepens in a way that you can't even begin to understand when you are standing at the beginning of it. I would never trade the love that we have now for those early years. It was amazing and exciting, and it was the thing that propelled us into this great love story. But nineteen years in, our souls are superglued together. They can never ever be separated. I describe the look in my husband's eyes that I never saw until he became a father. It is a look that draws me deeper in love with him. We have been through joys and sorrows. We have weathered storms and come out more grateful to be alive and together. I know this is forever love.

I can see gratitude in her eyes when I say this. Like all along she has been hoping that love doesn't have to fade away, even if that is what we are culturally conditioned to believe. I am reminded of the people who gave me this kind of hope when we were just starting out together. I will never forget the impact it made on me. And how it was a balm for my soul.

I am reminded of myself when I look at her. The uncomplicated version of myself—the one that is deep in thought over a journal with the right pen. The version of myself pre-children. The me that sees and feels deeply and has the ability to turn off all of the noise and distractions in life and just process and feel and write. I don't even try to articulate to her what a gift she has been given— uninterrupted thought. I know that it will be years before she can even begin to fathom what I am talking about. I notice all the things that are beautiful about her. And even though I don't know we are the same person, because we are alike in so many ways, I compare myself to her. The fresh haircut that frames her face, the vintage dress and Doc Martens, her easy, fluid way of talking. Her confidence. How pretty she looks. I am a little taken back by her zest for life, for ideas, for making a mark on the world. I am convicted by her passion. I think to myself that I want to be more like that.

She perks up when I tell her I am a writer. I explain that I don't have a lot of time to write, but that I am writing a book little by little, when I can make the time.

I told her that I love to bake. That I grind my own grain and make bread. She said that is something she has always wanted to learn. I tell her maybe I can teach her one day.

I tell her that my children are my friends. That they fill our house with music and laughter, and that they fill my life back up with wonder.

I get a text saying the baby needs me and tell her I better get going. She said that's best for her, too, because she has a big critique coming up in two days, and she has no idea what she's going to show. She is praying for a good idea, and she's going to stay here for a few more hours, brainstorming and trying to get inspired. I don't envy her.

I sense her gratitude that I've taken time to meet today. I can tell that she is trying to figure out her place in the world, that she is hungry for conversation about spiritual things, that her mind is working about what it is like to be a wife and mother and how to reconcile that with the calling that she feels God has put on her life. She is gathering data for what her life may become one day. She is seeing what works and what doesn't. She is making lists in her mind about her future. I understand. I do the same thing.

We exchange a hug and both say, at the same time, that we've so enjoyed getting together. I can tell she means it. I feel like I've learned something from her. And she feels the same about me.

Let's do this again sometime, I say.

She agrees.

I grab my journal, stuff it into my bag, wave goodbye, walk out to the car, and head back home to a houseful of people who love me. I feel rich. I feel alive.

I see her disappearing in my rearview mirror. And I think to myself, *I would never go back to 22.*

I take a deep, grateful breath and drive on home.

IN TIME
MAY 31, 2014

You can't slow it down. No matter how much you want this
moment of just-after-rain-shimmer, when the baby is still
sleeping and the kids are still in the backyard, preoccupied
with the change of the world under the influence of a spring
shower, you can't keep it. You can't stop it. You can't slow it
down. Even though the tea is hot and the mist on the breeze
tastes like honeysuckle. And you are surrounded by a chorus
of birdsong. Inevitably, what will happen is this: in a few
minutes, the sun will come out and suck up all the silver
shimmer from the streets. The baby will start to talk politely
in his crib. The kids will come up on the porch with legs of
solid mud.

You will have to get up and do something else.

You will go in and wash the red clay out of little boy clothes.
You will make dinner and begin the futile effort to sweep
clean the kitchen floor. You will oversee the brushing of 8
rows of teeth. You will try to make it go fast now. You will try
to rush through the diaper part and the jammies part and the
"I want a glass of water" part. But you can't speed it up. You
will have to patiently answer every question and soothe every
fear. No matter how much you push yourself to get it all over

with, there you are, looking for lost dollies. You say goodnight, take the stairs one by one, walk to the kitchen, and finish getting it cleaned up so that you can make breakfast in the morning.

The morning will be full of soft voices saying, "Good Moyn-ing, Mama", snuggles and little kisses and strong hugs. You will try to make this part last as long as you can.

This is my life. This is all the time in the world for me.

As of last week, Randy and I have been married for eleven years. I wrote out all the good memories I could think of on notebook paper to give to him. I just bawled like a baby, sitting there, summing up the 15 years we have known each other in little phrases on the page. There have been so many times we didn't know how we were going to make it. So many times when the future was a giant question mark. Looking back, it is like prophecy after prophecy being fulfilled. Promise after promise kept. Answers written with emphatic periods. Exclamation points. I can't believe how time has flown, and all along we have been carried on the wings of grace and mercy and unfailing love.

This morning we were telling our children what it means that God is faithful. It is easy to forget this, even when you have lived in seasons of miracles as we have. It means that His promises are true. And no matter what happens in this short span of life on earth, we can trust Him. Life is so beautiful and so terrible. The more beautiful it is, the more terrible it can be. He has a plan for making all of this right. And even when we are staring out into the cold, blank reality of the future before us, God has been there already. He goes before and behind. He hems us in. And it is going to be okay.

In time, the rain will cast its silver glow on everything again. The honeysuckle will die back but will come again next spring. There will be juicy blackberries and fragrant lavender blossoms in the meantime. The quiet moments will be few and far between, but there will be more little kisses and strong hugs and the contagious laughter of little children. We will fill page after page with the beautiful memories of this year and the next. Life will seem slow, but all the people in the grocery store tell me to enjoy it while I can, because these little ones will be grown in the blink of an eye.

We are not required to go fast or slow. Just to walk, step by step with the Spirit of God, not looking ahead in fear of the future, or looking back with regret for the past. To take one day at a time, trusting that there is a purpose to this life. That God is faithful. And that His promises are eternally true.

FOR WHICH MY HEART IS YEARNING
DECEMBER 3, 2020

In the busyness of the day, I forget that I am soul and spirit. I move, like a machine, through the mechanics of my life: head turning at a sudden cry, arms lifting baby, voice humming softly like a washing machine. Fingers folding laundry, hands scrubbing pots and pans, feet moving through rooms, ears listening, eyes taking in the light and explaining its meaning to my brain. I am a body in motion. Nothing more.

But in the holy hush of 4 a.m., I wake and realize that my heart is yearning. To live. To breathe. To have true being. To insert my soul and spirit into the frame of my body, to make them move in perfect synchronization. To enter deeply into the rhythms of my one-and-only life, wholeheartedly giving myself to the unassuming rituals that make up my days. I want to move gracefully around my life. To hear the clanking of dishes and the never-ending scuffle of bare feet and the irreplaceable human voices I love as exquisite, never-before-heard music. I want my body, soul, and spirit to respond as one. To make going through the motions a beautiful dance.

I want to find the beauty in my life. It is there, hidden. Today I will search for it. Today I will find that for which my heart is yearning.

LISTENING FOR THE SONG

MAY 6, 2015

Our baby is 3 months old now. We have settled into our new roles and are working ourselves into a more predictable pattern of living. Life as a mother of five small children is a blur. Every day has its own rhythm. Sometimes it is like a song. Sometimes it is total chaos.

Last week was particularly hard for me. I was sick with a fever for a couple of days. The whole time I kept waking up thinking, "Who is going to feed everybody?" Of course Randy took care of us. But laying in bed, I could feel the house getting more and more out of my control. I knew it was going to take me a long time to get on top of the monumental mess-making that was happening while my eyes were closed.

Sometimes, I just get completely overwhelmed by the amount of people living in this house. We weren't thinking about a family when we moved in. And we weren't expecting that it would be so hard to resell one day. And we certainly never dreamed we would have 5 children. We were short-sighted. We were writing songs and expecting to make a living making music, playing shows anytime and anywhere we were invited. It seemed like the greatest purpose of our lives. Something we had been working up to since we met. Something we would always do.

Life is different now. There are so many wonderful things about living with children. They are completely inspiring. (I say this while Rosie is sitting under the blossoming blackberry bushes, drawing the white flowers in her nature journal, and Paloma is sketching bright yellow dandelions and the tiny little lavender weed-flowers that are growing in our grass.) But there are times when I get so frustrated by how little I can find time to do. I grow weary of being the person who must ultimately meet the constant needs, who must address the constant interruption, who must answer the constant clamor of questions, who must think ahead for everyone. If I let myself think about all of the things I want to accomplish in life—things that, at one time, truly felt like the reason I was put on this earth—it will gnaw at me until I am completely discontent with the life I have been given.

My purpose has shifted. The person I used to be has been swept up into this powerful current that rushes day and night. These are the kind of waves that you can only take one by one, and you can not look too far ahead because they stretch out before you for miles. It takes faith to believe there is a calm ocean somewhere just beyond them.

This season will be over in a moment. I know this. Complete strangers tell me this almost every time I go to the grocery store. They tell me with regret and sadness in their voices. As if they truly wish they were the ones with two in the buggy and three at the waist. I know it is true. This little whisper of a moment where my baby laughs only by smiling will be a bittersweet memory in a few short weeks. The deepening color of fire-red hair, the morning sounds of running feet, the sharp surprise of every season shared with small children who are full of wonder. One day the house will be quiet. And I will miss the music in their voices. Oh how I love them. How I want to enjoy them every moment I can.

The purpose of my life is not to have more time. It is not to write songs or make things or update a blog. It is not to have an orderly house. It is not to live a life that is pleasant. It is not to do all of the things I have ever dreamed of. I am designed for one purpose, and it has very little to do with me. It is this: to love God, to know him, and bring him glory. This is what I want. This is the one thing that I can devote my life to without regret. The way this plays out is different now that I am a mother. I don't have to wake up in the morning and wonder what it is that I am supposed to do. I know. It starts with breakfast and it doesn't ever stop, not even when the last sleepy eye closes late in the evening. It is just to say yes to what God has begun in my life. To surrender to this season with my whole heart. To find joy in it. To listen for the song that lies beneath this chaos and to try, with all my heart, to sing along.

SURRENDERING TO A SEASON
OCTOBER 6, 2020

Today I drank a cup of tea for the first time in six weeks. Rich Assam with a swirl of cream. The taste of it brought tears to my eyes. It is October, and nothing complements the first of the crimsons and golds like a steaming mug of fragrant tea.

I am just rounding the corner on the first trimester of my ninth pregnancy. I cannot express to you what it means to me to wake up and feel alive, to want to get up out of bed, to have an appetite and actually *like* food, to enjoy being in the kitchen, to feel like I can genuinely smile at my children in the mornings, to have thoughts coming back into my head.

It has been an incredible and intense season of resting, waiting, listening, and ultimately surrendering to this all-consuming process again, which I have come to understand many times as a quiet calling that God is speaking over my life: to *allow another child to move through my body and into the world.*

The day before morning sickness hit me, I was literally sitting at my kitchen table with my journal, grateful, awestruck, teary-eyed, and overwhelmed by the flood of ideas that rushed through me. Every time I sat down in front of a blank page, words and lists and ideas would rush out of my pen. It was like the rainy season in Costa Rica, downpours out of clear skies, almost every single day of the week. I have not experienced creative flow like this since I became a mother thirteen years ago. My mind was awake, my thoughts were alive, and the words came down like a deluge. And I loved it.

I woke up to a pregnancy that turned my rushing-river of creative flow into barely-moving molasses. I would lay in bed for hours without a single thought in my head and just be dumbfounded by it. The juxtaposition was almost comical.

And slowly, over days and weeks of feeling that I had literally nothing to give to *anyone*, a few words came together as a phrase in my mind. And it comforted me.

This is what it means to surrender to a season.

Surely nothing has taught me how to surrender more than motherhood, which has left no part of my life untouched.

This is what a mother does: she surrenders her life to the different seasons of serving her family. She is constantly learning to lay aside her own preferences, her own wants and desires, for the sake of her beloved children. Through pregnancy she offers up her body as an empty vessel that will carry a life over the wide ocean to the other side of the womb. She offers her mind, which is overtaken by the needs of her children and making visionary plans to serve her family. She offers her soul, which is knit so deeply together with these lives that have moved through her body that the cost is dear.

And this is precious to God. This is my worship. For the last six weeks, it hasn't appeared inspiring or praise-worthy. It looks like laying on a bed. It looks like sleeping through the heavy hours of morning-and-afternoon sickness. It looks like letting a lot of non-essentials go. It looks like allowing myself to be served. Allowing my husband and older children to pick up my responsibilities for a season. And to be ok with that. Because God is doing this work in their lives too. And the truth is, there is no other way for this perfect tiny, imperceptible heart to be formed and begin to beat than to surrender to the whole process. The discipline of rest. The discipline of surrender. The discipline of trust. The discipline of saying yes to the next step and following through with faith.

There is beauty in every season. Just as the leaves are beginning to golden, I feel the glow of life stirring in me. I feel the plum-sized baby moving in my womb. And I feel myself waking up to the joy of it. Waking up to the beauty of a new season. I am tasting tea for the first time again. I am seeing the early light of the morning with childlike surprise and new wonder. I feel alive. Awake anew to the miracle and sacred beauty of my one-and-only life.

And as this season changes, with a heart full of gratitude, again, I surrender.

MY DAUGHTER PLAYS THE PIANO

My daughter plays the piano and I am carried through time. I hear the first chorded cry, after the lifesong of her body broke open my womb and burst forth like a melody. Our voices, separate, but blended as one.

The movement of her youth has passed. A lively staccato that made us dance and laugh. A twirling girl, a song to be carried on your shoulders. A springing singing, sweetly ringing, filling up the room. Allegro.

And the music changes and brings me back to this moment. Here she sits, at piano's edge, a young woman. A slow adagio. A lilting, lullabied theme, the phrases lengthening, tremulous and sweet. And I listen.

Life is a passing song. Measure by measure, we are asked to open our hearts to it. To let it touch us. To let it move us. To let it change us from the inside out.

My daughter plays the piano, and in my heart, I sing along.

THE SACRED EVERYDAY
OCTOBER 31, 2018

This morning I woke up to a miracle.

All of my children are still soundly sleeping in their beds,
except for the baby, who came down early to snuggle. Her
head is fuzzy and soft like a little duck. The house is dark. And
quiet. There is no birdsong yet. The hum of thought in the
back of my mind has not yet been interrupted by small voices
asking for breakfast.

I open my eyes. And they see.

And it is a miracle.

I take a deep, solid breath of morning air. I am alive.

In all of history, out of all the souls that have inhabited the
bodies of people who have since been remembered or forever
forgotten, today my heart is beating.

Today the rituals of motherhood have meaning. This day is
not about trying and failing to get something accomplished,
pushing back my own desires to meet one need after the
other all day long. This day is about seeing the light reflected

in the eyes of my living children. It is about their hair, which we call red or brown, but is really a million different hidden colors that reveal themselves slowly through varying intensities of sunlight. It is the unforgettable smell of a little baby. It is the feeling of one hand lightly touching another. This day is about the sound of voices—the absolute irreplaceability of the music that comes from each one. It is about the words that rise up and fill this house full to the brim each day. It is the taste of freshly baked muffins and coffee around a table with the people that I love and most-cherish in this world.

Life is a sacred gift.

Today, and with all my heart, I will receive it.

Standing in the Hallway

of Sorrow

MISS AND CARRY

MAY 2018

I miscarried nine days before our 15th anniversary. There we sat, across the table at a little cafe, drinking coffee together. Our six living children were home with a friend who gave us the day together to celebrate our marriage.

The week before, Randy and I had privately laid the whisper of a body down in the ground in a secret spot in the woods, under a y-shaped tree, marked by a heart-shaped stone. The ground was covered with a green carpet of fan clubmoss, which seemed almost friendly, and the forest was mottled with sunshine like something straight out of a Miyazaki movie.

I was nine days out from what was the greatest tragedy of my blessed life. The thing that actually happened. Small in comparison to what many have been called to suffer in losing children or loved ones, but I could feel the cold, sharp wind of grief blowing right through me.

We went for a hike to Hemlock Falls. It was beautiful. The falls were majestic. The sound of rushing water was like a mother singing a lullaby. I was comforted by the strength and the voice of the waters. It reminded me that I am small.

We got in the car and started driving down the mountain. We listened to the album of songs we recorded four years earlier. They all felt different. All the lyrics I ever sang carried another thread of meaning now. I wept.

Mis-Carry. I don't like this word. It implies that I carried this baby differently. But I didn't. My womb had an open door, the baby came in, and I accepted the life with the same fear and trembling, the same joy and wonder, the same gentle reminder that God is the creator and sustainer of life and that all I have to do is trust him and live and breathe. I carried the baby in my heart and in my body with the same faith in a loving and merciful God.

When we told the kids we were having a baby, their joy was uncomplicated and perfect. Our oldest burst into tears almost before I got the words out of my mouth. The oldest three children spontaneously ran to smother me with hugs. The youngest three asked questions. We answered them with laughter and hearts full of hope.

We talked about baby names. We started making plans. I carried this baby with an uncomplicated and trusting love, with peace and hope and a rooted faith in the same God who had delivered babies into my arms before.

So what did I miss?

Miscarry is not a good enough word for the physical separation of two souls. It doesn't explain how deep the wound goes. It doesn't begin to describe what it is like to cry with your whole body. To cry in blood. It doesn't describe the emptiness that lingers when the little house is swept clean and in order and no one is home.

I told my husband I was shocked by how much this hurts. We had barely known of the existence of this little soul. Only a few short weeks. He looked me in the eyes and told me that I was nurturing and nourishing this child for 10 weeks, keeping it alive with my own body. He told me I am this baby's mother.

I am this baby's mother.

That is a comfort to me. And it somehow explains why it is okay to let myself feel every difficult, confusing, sorrowful emotion that I feel. Even though this tiny life was just a flicker. This child is mine.

I am grateful that when we told our children we would not get to meet our baby this side of Heaven, they sobbed. I didn't want to tell them because I didn't want them to cry. But I am grateful for their sorrow, because it proves that the life that came and went so quickly was treasured and loved and wanted. That their love and hope for that child was pure and sweet and good and a gift from God. And I think we all sense that we are blessed to mourn, for we are truly finding comfort in the arms of Christ.

As I am writing this, I am wrapped in a shawl given to me by a dear friend who lives across the country. It is a comfort to me. Our 18-month-old's little round pink cheeks and her chubby little fingers that pull at my elbows is a comfort to me. Friends and family who step in and take over my life so I can heal and get some rest—what an incredible comfort. Meals, messages, texts, prayers for our family. The word of God. These things comfort me. The indescribable beauty of the faces of my living children. What a miracle it is to see them before me. What an immeasurable gift this life is. I know that I am not alone and that God is with us.

I believe that this tiny flicker of a life, though the little candle has now gone out, has a purpose. It has a purpose in this life and in the life to come, which is all the same life. Life is everlasting. And though we suffer because we will not see the face of this child in the only life we understand—here on this earth—we have hope and peace that this child is in the presence of our loving God. And that one day, we will know this child as our own. I am grateful that our little one is finished with suffering and pain. And I trust that God will use the life of this child as a seed that is planted here on earth. A seed that will grow and flourish and bear fruit. Even in death, God causes new life to spring up. I pray that over this little one.

And though I ache to know our baby on this earth, I will continue to carry the comforting knowledge that this child was and is. And I think in that way, the word, miscarry, serves me. For as long as I live, I will both miss and carry this child in my heart.

STANDING IN
THE HALLWAY OF SORROW

(In honor of my beautiful, selfless mother who went home to be with Jesus November 3, 2019, hours after I wrote these words.)

I am going to write something that is braver and stronger than I now feel, but I believe it with all my heart.

Daddy met Mama on a Sunday morning at a little church. She was singing that day. His first impression of her was, I'm sure, her beauty and her voice.

Last night I listened to an old voicemail from Mama. All it said was, "Hey Mackenzie. Give me a call when you get a chance. Love you." I sent it to myself as an email so it didn't get accidentally deleted from my phone. I love that voice.

It is early Sunday morning. I am waking up, lying in bed before the sun has come up, wanting to call my sisters but not wanting to wake them. I am wondering if the thing that I feared most in the early years of my childhood has happened in the night. Did I lose my Mama?

I remember never leaving her side. I held her hand, clung to her, sat beside her when she played the piano in church—

because sitting in the pews was like sitting on the other side of the ocean. I remember crying my eyes out when she dropped me off for school because I was so afraid something would happen and she wouldn't make it back to get me.

I couldn't bear the thought of my life without her.

She has had a year of great trials and suffering. Through it all, she has remained beautiful and gracious, strong beyond belief, with a faith that has risen up pure and true and has carried her with peace to the very threshold of this earthly life.

I expect, and even hope, that by morning, she will be gone to Jesus.

In the days and hours leading up to death, there are two words that keep offering themselves back to me: fear and regret.

I refuse them both.

I refuse to look ahead and fear what is going to happen. How much suffering she will endure. How much we will lose. How deep the ache will go when she is separated from her body and we are left in a wide chasm of loss. I have to shut this door. Slam it shut. I will not walk into the chamber of fear. Life is too short and too precious to waste valuable time in anxiety over what may, and even very-likely-will happen. This moment is the moment that counts. This is the one where I have the explosive power of choice. Where breath carries meaning, and the words spoken change the atmosphere.

I refuse to open the door of my future to fear. And I refuse to leave the doors behind me open to regret.

Yes, we could have done things differently. I wish I would have written down more of Mama's stories. I wish I had recorded her singing and playing the piano. I wish I had more than this two-sentence voicemail to remember that beautiful, musical way that she spoke to me before she had to slip inside herself to begin the process of dying. I wish I would have *been there* more. I wish I would have made that one last trip happen. I wish that I had given my children more time to make memories with her in her last days. I wonder if we made all the right choices regarding her care when she was sick. Did we push where we should have just let go? What would have happened if. . . These are the questions that can haunt like ghosts. They can poison like cancer. But in the face of great sorrow, I have a choice. I am choosing to walk forward from here, knowing that we have prayed over every major decision of our lives, trusting that God is leading us, that He helped us make the right decisions at the time, and for where we have misstepped or misheard his voice, there is abundant, redeeming grace. He is able to wrap everything up with details that show his infinite love, compassion, and mercy.

Wishing for a past that never existed is the greatest waste of this precious moment that we are now living. I refuse to allow regret to rob me of the riches of this life.

I will hear Mama's angelic voice again. I will hear it as never before in Heaven. And even on this earth, I will hear the echoes of her voice, as her children and grandchildren gather around the living room to sing her favorite hymns. So many voices. . . A choir singing harmony, all derived from the same genetic pair of voices. She is in the voice of my own children. The song of our family goes on and on and on. . .

In the hallway of sorrow, I choose to walk into the room where there is music. To sing this song as my mother has bravely shown me all my life. Not looking ahead in fear, not looking back with regret, but entering into each moment, one grateful breath at a time.

BEING THERE
(ON THE SHORES OF LIFE AND LOSS)
NOVEMBER 2019

A week ago we cried over the body of my beloved mother. *She is gone.* This keeps hitting me like ocean waves, one after the other. How it swells. How it breaks.

It all seems like a dream. The next day was, of course, a birthday. My daughter's third. The only time to cry was into the birthday cake batter or at the Dollar Store, when a stranger smiled, counted my seven children and said, "Are they all yours?" Thinking of my beautiful, humble mother who had nine, I said yes, looked away, and wiped tears from my face.

One day it's Amazing Grace around the gravesite, the next it's Happy Birthday around the kitchen table. I can hardly process this metaphor.

After church last Sunday, I mourned and celebrated the life of my mother by loading up the kids with a van full of luggage and art supplies and to-go bags and snacks, and we drove to the beach. I understood Mama in a new way taking this many little people to see the ocean, which after God and her family, was maybe her next greatest love. What a comical mess and heroic struggle to get everyone there and back home again.

But being there. . .

Oh, being there.

Being there.

Standing on the shore of the ocean with my family is one of the purejoy-est moments I have ever experienced in my life. These kids don't care it's mid-November. They are wet from head to toe. They are laughing and freezing, falling, running, jumping, soaking in every glorious sea-salt-blue-sky-sunshine-shimmery moment. They take every wave. One by one.

Being there.

Being there is worth the what-should-have-been a five-hour car drive. It's worth the two solid days of packing and the week of recovery and reorganizing life after coming home. It's worth the sand and the spills and the stops and starts. The ocean fills us up with wonder. We feel small. We feel grateful to be alive. We aren't doing anything else right now. We are just 100% being there.

Being there.

Life is hard.

It aches. The heart breaks in waves.

Standing in the sea, on the shore of this world, I am longing for the next where there is no sadness or suffering or pain. Where lives that are hand-stitched lovingly together are not ripped apart at the seams.

It would be easy to drown in this kind of sorrow. To walk down into the waters of regret, to be pulled under by the currents of fear for the future of my own children who must one day feel what I feel today.

I loved my mother's laughter, her beautiful, gentle voice, her instantaneous "yes" to ideas of adventure. I will most miss her understanding eyes, the smile that always met me at the front door, the way she made my life easy, carefree, uncomplicated, and full of things that were beautiful. The way she let me become myself, always walking alongside me. Never pushing, but putting things along the path for me to discover. I miss seeing Mama and Daddy as a matching set and saying their names together. I mourn all the little ways she made me know I was loved.

But I am still here. And I have little ones who look to me as I have always looked to my own mother for love and comfort. What a miracle to see them before me. The sets of eyes, the faces alive with every emotion, the indescribable brilliance of red and brown hair in sunshine. . . The hearts that are tender, touched by first sorrow. The feeling of standing beside them, knowing we share something that can never be recreated: *mother and child*. The beauty of being here with the ones I love moves me profoundly. The voice of the wind and water is a lullaby. Achingly beautiful. Hauntingly sweet. I am standing in the wake of an ocean that is deep and wide, calm and wild, brutal and brave and brimming over with lifesong.

Traveling the long road is hard. There are so many places along the way where we didn't want to stop but we had to. To get to this moment. I see that my love for my children is even now deepening because of these waves of sadness and loss. I wouldn't want it any other way. How tragic it would be to lose a mother and feel nothing. How grateful I am to have had a mother who gently led me here with love and grace. Even though it was she who was truly suffering, she held my hand and walked me calmly, bravely to the door of my own grief.

Life aches. But being here is worth it.

I renounce fear. I refuse regret. I wear my sorrow like a shawl wrapped gently around my shoulders. It is a bittersweet comfort but it doesn't choke the life out of me. It reminds me of what I've lost, but it doesn't keep me from embracing those who are standing in this ocean with me. Like a child on the shore, I take one wave at a time and concentrate on breathing, on showing up for the beauty, on waking up to the love that is alive all around me.

Just breathing.

Just being.

Being there.

My Beautiful Dying Mother, A Birth Story

November 27, 2019

Mama had nine children. I am the youngest, and I have often felt a deep sense of gratitude that she surrendered her life to this process so many times. I see it as no small miracle that I even exist in the world. And that my seven children exist.

Mama was always the first person I would call when I went into labor. She and Daddy slept with their shoes at the foot of the bed so they could hop right into them in the middle of the night, rush over to my house, and take care of all my little ones while I went to the hospital. I always *loved* calling her when the baby was finally born and the hard work was over. She understood exactly what I was feeling and even more. She shared my joy as a woman, a Mama, and a Grandma. She would say to me, "Oh, I know you are *so relieved*. I am *so happy* for you, Mackenzie."

I could hear the smile in her beautiful, singular, unique-in-this-world voice. We talked about how the moment after the baby is born is *the best feeling in the whole world*.

There is no relief like it. She said that she remembered waking up the day after having a baby, thinking she was still pregnant, and all of the sudden remembering she was already done and the baby was born. *And how happy she was to be on the other side.*

Standing at the bedside of my beautiful, dying mother, I could not help but notice how like birth death can be. Her husband and children surrounded her like nurses and midwives. We attended her needs and tried to make her as comfortable as possible—a sip of water, a word of encouragement, whispered prayers. We watched for the signs of labor progressing—the changes in her breathing, the deep and intense focus on an inner struggle, the changing expressions of her beautiful, rapidly-aging face. We sang hymns around her bedside as she actively labored.

Over the years, I have had many conversations about birth with Mama. I asked her if she was ever afraid. She said that in labor, she always tried to be calm because she knew if she was afraid, the baby would be afraid. I know she didn't want us to be afraid of death. Just as she didn't want us to be afraid of birth. That is why, with God's grace, she walked this whole difficult road with such beauty, composure, love, and tenderness. She was showing us that there is nothing to fear in dying. She knew if she was afraid, we would be afraid, too.

I remembered those words while I stood beside her, watching her walk bravely through the valley of the shadow of death. Her calm was a comfort to us. Even in dying, she was showing us how to live with selfless love and grace.

When I would come home from the hospital, new baby in my arms, Mama was always there to welcome me home. She had taken care of my children, somehow managed to do my laundry and clean my kitchen, and left me with a hot meal for dinner. She would say, "*I know you are so glad to be home.*" And then she would tell me that she always thought the hardest part of having a baby was leaving all of her children behind when she had to go to the hospital.

She didn't want to leave us. I know this is why she hung on so long though her suffering was intense. She needed to know we were settled, that we were going to be ok. I know this is what she was thinking the last year of her life. She knew how we would all miss her. How our lives would never be the same without her. She, who had always tried to make our lives as simple, as free from sadness and pain as possible, would be the one whose passing would leave a lasting impression upon us.

We stood around her, singing praise songs, laughing and crying, speaking love over her life, remembering the past aloud so that she could hopefully hear us from wherever deep inside herself she might be.

I imagined her lying in a bed like this, 38 years ago, when her body was young and strong, but wracked with a parallel, all-consuming helplessness of laboring through transition. Where all of her focus was on staying alive and making it through the long and hard delivery that brought about my birth.

Our sweet mama. She opened her eyes and we all gathered around her, quietly, lovingly, through tears cheering her on. It was the crowning, the ring of fire where the soul exits the body. Though her body labored and died, her spirit was the child that was born into new life. The passing of her soul from this world to everlasting life was such a holy birth.

I felt a surge of relief when she died. Not unlike the relief I have felt when giving birth. It was a great ocean-wave of gratitude to God that the hard work was over. I sat on the floor and wept and praised God for his mercy, thanking him that she was free from the suffering of this life. It was like the relief of birth without the laughter and fullness of joy.

We could only experience the great relief that her suffering was over. But how alive she must have felt. How free from the cares of this world. How exquisitely she must have sensed the love in which there is no fear or sadness or even a tinge of sorrow. No bitter, only sweet. Where the love of a mother becomes complete—the work of her life completely done. The joy was on the other side. Full joy. Complete joy. Everlasting.

I will always be grateful to my mother, who walked out a sweet and steadfast life of faith. She walked me through death as she walked me through birth and through life—with great love, gentleness, and courage. This is the lasting impression her passing has made on me.

I know she is so relieved. And though my heart aches to see her again in this world, I am so glad that she is home.

FIRST BIRTHDAY
(LOVE SONG FOR A BABY)
MAY 21, 2020

You came to me from a distant land,
the secret place of my innermost being.
You traveled miles and miles to find me.

You came in the space
between my two greatest sorrows.
When the lamp of my womb went out, suddenly
leaving me with a cold-wind feeling,
like the door to every chamber of my heart
had been left blowing open
on a long, dark, winter night,
your little life brought light and warmth
and joy, welling up.

I sang through your birth.
In the raging waters,
I reached up for mercy with song
and the hand of God reached back
and pulled me out of the storm
and set my feet to walk upon the waters.

I could never explain to you what it meant to me
to hold you in my arms and close to my heart
as I stood with my brothers and sisters
around the bed of my beautiful, dying mother.

You gave me courage and hope
and a reason to be brave.
to laugh and cry at the same time.
Your little head, resting on my chest
was a comfort that could penetrate
the heaviness of grief.
When I lingered too deeply
in the waters of sorrow,
that look in your dear little eyes
could call me instantly back home.

You are a miracle.
Your life is the thread
in the hand of God
stitching these hollow aching holes closed.

I longed, years, to see your face.
I traveled far to find you.
Your name was a whispered prayer,
a secret longing,

a hope that kept me going
when I thought I could not go on.

And now you are here,
quietly sleeping in the other room.
A promise kept,
a hope fulfilled.

Happy birthday
beautiful, beautiful boy.
You will wake to bright balloons and song.

GRIEF IS A RIVER
JANUARY 3, 2020

Grief is a river that now runs through my life. Sometimes it is slow and steady, passing gently over rocks of remembrance, pooling up in beautiful, idyllic scenes where the late afternoon sun brushes through the trees and paints the waters and the riverbank in bright splashes of quivering light. The aching beauty of having loved.

The memory of my mother's elegant hands—folding laundry, soothing a fever, throwing a snowball, washing dishes, painting with watercolors, brushing her hair, playing hymns on the piano, drinking a Coke, pulling up a blanket, driving a car, signing a permission slip, putting on lipstick, playing cards, waving in her singsong way, washing my hair in the kitchen sink, scrubbing the floor, holding my hand in a parking lot, animating her speech, making a birthday cake, turning the pages of a children's book, touching my shoulder, wiping my tears. . . These are the little rocks that it rolls over, slow and steady, calm and bitterly sweet.

Sometimes the waters run like a flood—a dam broken, a waterfall of sorrow. The tragedy of having deeply loved and lost.

The empty spaces in photographs and at the Christmas table. The phone call that didn't come this year on my birthday. Old home videos and text messages and the finality of death in this life. Mothering while grieving and feeling wrong for not having time to let myself properly mourn.

But there are gifts of grace I feel while grieving my mother's life. I know she understood what it means to allow children to work on every part of you—your joys and sorrows, your hopes and plans, every sleeping and waking moment of your whole life. I feel her presence profoundly in her absence.

And so I sit in the beauty of the day and watch the light reflecting off the moving waters. I let my children splash in it when I can. I do my best to pull them up out of the current before the rapids take us all under. There is beauty here and danger and a reckoning with the wild ways of nature. Things will never be the same now that we know waters have this kind of power.

So we lean in close together and whisper a prayer of thanks for the gift of breath in our lungs and hearts that are beating. We cling to the hope that there is another side to life. One we can't see yet but that is more familiar to us now that the face of someone we dearly love is waiting for us there. We breathe. We breathe. We breathe. We hold as tightly as we can to those we love while trying to hold them loosely, knowing that they belong, not to us, but to our tender, ever-loving and gracious God.

It is such a gift to be alive. To have loved and to love and to walk the banks of the sweet and wild river hand in hand.

BROKEN OPEN-HEARTED LOVE
APRIL 22, 2020

Yesterday I learned that a dear friend is dying. There is no time to visit. No time to wrap up loose ends. This news just rips it all back open—that wound that I thought was nearly healed. The blow from my fall where I realized that death is actually a part of the human story. My story. The story of those that I love.

This hurts.

How singular and rich and inimitable one voice can be. All the music of it. The deep, lyrical, easiness of speech. The words forming phrases and sentences and conversations that are uniquely alive in the moment and then are replayed as memories. Laughter that starts in the eyes and crescendos into an unforgettable song.

How priceless it is to sit around a table with someone that you love and eat homemade pizza and listen to a true story, directly from the mouth of the one who lived it. With embellishments. With exaggerations. With hand motions and emphatic pauses. What an indescribable gift it is to look across a room and see a friend drinking coffee. Alive. Responding. Speaking as if singing. Breathing as if praying.

What a blessed, beautiful gift it is to have life and breath. To speak. To sing. To laugh. To cry. To think. To feel. To remember. To love deeply and be loved in return.

I just cannot get over how beautiful life is. My heart is broken over it.

In the stark reality of loss, I am awake, more than ever, to the miracle of ordinary life. I walk forward into that as bravely as I know how.

On this side of eternity, this moment is all that I have with the ones I hold dear. There is no time for fear or regret. There is no time for bitterness or unforgiveness. In this life, there is only time for decisive, courageous, and open-hearted love.

GRIEF AND THE PATH OF BEAUTY
NOVEMBER 17, 2020

Let me start by saying I do not pretend to be an expert on grief, and I truly hope I never *am* an expert on grief. My life has been colored by it just enough for me to know that this is something that's going to stay with me forever. And that it is worth thinking about and wrestling with, because it is going to continue to be a part of my story. These are my own humble thoughts and observations about grief, and I offer them up as a friend, sitting at the kitchen table, over a cup of coffee, with more questions than answers, in hopes that together we may find some words that can anchor us to hope in the wide, wild sea of loss in earthly life.

Grief is surprising. I didn't know how deep a hollow ache could go through me until I lost a child to miscarriage. I didn't know if there was a back wall to the cavern that opened up inside my heart, or if that cold-wind-feeling would just blow through me forever. I didn't know if I would ever stop crying at the breakfast table, or in the bathroom, or driving in the car. At any moment, a look, a word, a thought, a touch could transport me out of my beautiful life and into the hollow darkness of grief.

But grief changed. The surprise became less sharp and severe. The heavy sorrow lifted and gave way to a beautiful hope that life on earth is not all there is. I will forever be grateful for the memory of that profound feeling of loss. Because it showed me a depth to love that I did not understand before. I take comfort in knowing that I am that sweet tiny baby's mother, and that little one is my child. And not even death can separate what God has put together.

I recognized the feeling, instantly, again, in the days leading up to my own mother's death. Different because this time, I was losing someone with whom I had a deep and rich history. Someone with a familiar name, a lyrical voice, a bright and easy laugh. The first arms that ever held me. The intimate soul who stood by me through every season of my entire life, lovingly and gently allowing me to become myself. Praying for me, encouraging me, blessing my life with her sweet and selfless love. Losing my mother brought a different sorrow, but the same hollow ache. That iconic scene in a movie where you are standing on the high edge of a deep canyon, screaming, "NOOOOOOOOOOOOOOO!" and falling to your knees as the thing you love descends in slow motion below the clouds and out of view forever.

Grief stays with us. It doesn't just go away. A year later, I realize this. I still want to talk to Mama. I miss her gentleness, her ability to listen, her soft-spoken words of guidance. I grieve that my son, now 18 months old, will not remember her. And that she will not be there to welcome the baby in my womb into this world. I miss her in the thoughts of the upcoming holidays. And even though my hope in heaven is secure, and I know I will see her again one day, I cannot deny the bleak reality that two lives, lovingly stitched together, can and eventually will be severed for earthly-ever. The finality of death in this life. I'm sure I will never get over this. How a person can be there one day, telling a story, laughing, crying, making plans. And the next day, they are gone.

I have wrestled with knowing how to even respond to grief. I can't run away from it. I certainly don't want to drown in the deep waters of it. But somehow, I know that it is something I must learn to allow God to use in my life. I don't embrace death or loss or despair or sorrow, because I believe we were made to live in a world where these things do not exist. And that one day, we will. But I do want to embrace grief as a teacher and a guide. As painful as it is, I cannot deny that it deepens my gratitude for all the love that remains in my life, and it waters the seed of hope that this life is surely not the end of my story. I believe that grief can lead us down a path of beauty, if we can walk with her. Not looking ahead in fear over what more we can and almost certainly will one day lose. Not looking behind, regretting all the experiences that were taken from us because we lost what we loved too soon. But to take a steady pace of deep thankfulness that there is love, that we have known it, and that love endures forever. To walk forward in this, one sacred step at a time.

I know that grief has led me into profound beauty. The way that I wrap my own children up, pull them close, linger longer around the table to talk or on the couch with a good book. The pure joy I have found in my little son, who filled my empty, aching womb with the spark of life and love again. The gratitude I feel, in the absence of my dear mother, for the memories of her beautiful life, for her likeness that I see in my brothers and sisters. For the words and songs and habits that she planted in my heart. In her absence, I am more grateful than ever to have had her presence in my life.

I find deep joy and comfort in the women who have stepped in to love, encourage, and mentor me in this past year. Surely this is a gift I once took for granted.

Seeing the world as one who has lost deeply can give us a heightened awareness of the ephemeral luster of the ordinary details of our lives. A cup of coffee, a morning shared with a friend, the face of a child. The moon, the stars, sitting by the fire. Color, music, words, living conversation, the touch of a hand. Voice. Breath. The life that is in the body. Awake for this moment in history to tell a singular story. The lives of those we love intertwined in a narrative that has an end here on earth, but a secret, sacred to-be-continued in eternity.

Grief doesn't go away. But I believe she can walk gently with us, putting her arm around our shoulders, taking us down a path that leads us to see beauty in this life and in the life to come.

THE MEMORY
OF AN UNEXPECTED RAIN

The time we left the little house
In a whispering rain
And ran to the shore,
Umbrellas in hand
I became, again, a child,
My daughters, dearest friends
We three, splashing, fully dressed
In the lapping waves
And laughing.

The experience I imagined in full sun
Sand glittering, shore shining,
A perfect day at sea,
Dimmed, bending to the
Shimmery silver and muted beauty
Of an unexpected rain.

Every Morning I Wake
in an Ocean

Every Morning
I Wake In An Ocean
December 28, 2020

Every morning I wake in an ocean. Sometimes the waters are calm, sometimes they are tumultuous, raging with storms that seem to never subside. They are always over my head. It is easy to slip under the waters of fear. It is effortless to drown in downpours of sorrow. It is second-nature to be swallowed whole by waves of regret and fall to the bottom of the dark sea, lying motionless, unable to breathe or speak or love. It is natural to wake, gather all of my strength, and tread water, pushed in on every side by the never-ending needs that break about me like ocean waves. But every morning, I make a choice to swim to the shore and live.

I open my eyes to the great expanse of God's love. Breath by breath, I hold fast to the strength of God's promises. I battle fear with faith that God is sovereign. I daily deal it the final blow, leaving it sinking to the depths of the sea. Stroke by stroke, I speak to my sorrowful heart with hope, reminding myself that this life is only a glimpse of the life to come. That all we have lost will be restored beyond what our mortal minds can even begin to comprehend. That these waves of great sadness will not last forever. I leave my sorrows in the great wide sea and move towards the golden shore, where the sun is opening a glorious new day before me. I swim and silence the voices of the waters of regret that crash around me by singing songs of God's steadfast love and deep forgiveness. My God and Savior, whose mercies never come to an end. They are new every morning.

Every morning I wake in an ocean. And every morning, it is the strong arms of faith, hope, and love that guide me to the shore, where I stand. And live. And breathe. And love. And move through my life with meaning and purpose. On the shore, I wake to the beauty around me. The colors of sunrise, the taste of coffee, the breath in my lungs, the hearts that beat in the bodies of those I love, the hopeful face of a child, the lilting vibrations of a piano, the music of voice, the smell of bread baking, the walk to the mailbox, the unexpected sighting of a perfectly synchronized flock of birds, the orchestra of nature, the touch of a friend, the first snow, the light behind the eye, cold water, warm coat, two hands woven together, the flicker of a candle, laughter that doesn't want to stop.

Every morning I wake in an ocean of fear, of sorrow, of regret, of overwhelm, of the ache and struggle of earthly life. And every day I make a choice to swim to the shore and live. Because every day begins with a morning that is rich with the new mercies of God's deep and abiding, steadfast love.

BRIDGE TO PEACE

Can I be honest? Sometimes my everyday life does not feel sacred. Sometimes the music of my life sounds more like noise than song. Existence is exhausting. It feels routine in the most uninspired way. Drained of joy and beauty. Life feels like hard work that is never-ever-ever-ever going to get done. It feels scary. Like a run-on question with no mark at the end. And not anything like the picture in my head when I was young and full of wonder and signing binding contracts on my future.

There, I said it.

The fact that my husband and I are raising a family of eight children in this increasingly angry, turbulent society, making a modest living in the middle of a shut-down-the-world-pandemic would be laughable if it wasn't so terrifying.

But the truth of the matter is this: I wake up every day and choose how I want to look at my life. This is a power that is given to me. And I'm not going to lie: sometimes, the choice is hard. It is easy to get sucked into a life of worry and anxiety over the future. It is easy to want to run and hide from the responsibility I've gotten myself into. To want to temporarily hand my life over to someone who is more qualified than I am to meet the needs of all people who count on me to survive. It is easy to drown in the ocean of needs that hit and beat and break, wave after wave, low-tide, high-tide, day and night, night and day and wonder how we will ever rise to the surface. The strong, silent current that sweeps up every hope and pulls it under. I have been in this place. And there is no way to breathe when you are living in those waters.

It is just as easy to go through the motions of your life while in your heart you are questioning every decision you ever made that got you here. You sit and stare in the mirror of the past, wondering if the image before you is the best that could have come from your life. And you lose yourself there, becoming nothing more than your own shadowy reflection. A thing that no one can touch or feel or hold close.

God, I don't want to live like that.

Every day these choices are offered to me. Live in fear. Live in regret.

I refuse. I refuse. I refuse.

Because I know that, no matter how I may feel, my life really is sacred. That is the truth. My life is a gift. It has meaning and purpose and a holy weight to it because I was created in the image of God for his glory. And even when it feels hard and confusing and overwhelming and the future is one huge question that I cannot answer, it is ok. Because I have the power to make a choice. I can live in fear or regret, or I can choose to walk a bridge to peace.

I walk that bridge through prayer, reflection, and the creative process. And all of this takes place on the pages of my journal. Journaling is the way I think, feel, process, and understand my life. When I move my hand across the blank page, my thoughts become words, my words become ink, and that ink reveals to me what is in my heart. It shows me my thoughts with stark clarity. I can see them for what they are. I can take them captive. I can lean into them or let them go. I can send them up as a prayer. I can move beyond the shadows and begin to live in a way that connects me to the true purpose and meaning for which I was created. I can see the beauty around me for what it is. Each season with its own exquisite joys. Each day its own grand symphony, never to be replayed, but to be enjoyed fully, completely, for one magnificent performance.

In my journal, I am able to sift through the noise and hear the melody line of my one and only life. And it is here, in words scrawled by my own humble hand, God teaches me to embrace my song and sing it with surrender.

THE STORY OF YESTERDAY
SEPTEMBER 21, 2017

This is the story of yesterday. Yesterday is recurring in this household. It is a day that starts way before I am ready to get up and ends way later than I want to stop. It starts with babies crying that they want to eat and get up and it ends with babies crying that they are not tired and don't want to go to bed.

Yesterday is the day that I wake up thinking about how irreplaceable I am. How could my family even survive a day without me? How many days would it take me to recover what little order remains if I were to take a day off. . . On yesterdays, I am constantly aware of how needed I am. I am the one everyone wants to talk to. I am the one who answers the questions. Constant interruption. Constant interruption. I wished that I'd never even thought of that phrase in its relationship to parenting.

I try in vain to find a few minutes to myself. All day long. Every time, I get more frustrated. Because there is not enough time in the day to do a fraction of anything.

I wrestle with my identity. I wrestle with my purpose. I wrestle with the person I have become.

I think about the book I want to write. I set that dream right beside the one where my house is clean and in order. Where the laundry is done.

And I go back into the kitchen to clean up or make the next meal.

This is the story of yesterday.

***

This is the story of today.

Today I woke up to the softest, sweetest little human voice in all the world. And she is calling for me. And I am the best thing in the world to her. I pick her up, nurse her, try for a few more minutes of rest feeling the glow in my heart of having a little baby right there beside me. Her little tiny fingers. Her delight that it is morning and we are awake. The first smile of the day.

Today there is good coffee and cranberry muffins and talk about the first day of fall which will be coming soon. The table is alive with the faces of six beautiful children. There is humming at the table! The unrehearsed symphony of voices at breakfast. This particular song will never be heard again. It is just for this meal, this moment.

I catch a glimpse of my husband across the table and feel gratitude that this is my life and we made it this far, and that we have accomplished something much greater than the book I wanted to write or the fleeting dream of a spotless, always-guest-ready house.

The day progresses with a routine schedule, but I am really there. I am not fighting against the rituals of housework or schoolwork, because they are rich with meaning. These are the moments that, one by one, are making up our lives. There are the slanted loops of written letters, my girls' laughing voices, thousands of tiny bits of paper on the floor. There are doll dresses and piano songs, train tracks and math facts, the indescribable beauty of sunshine on red hair. There is constant conversation about books and bugs and baking. Words fill up this house to the ceiling every day before they expire and clear for the following. But today I listen. I see that my girls are changing and growing. I notice how beautiful they have become. I hear that my boys think in ways I never would have imagined. I hear the dear, beautiful music of a two year old's voice. I see the baby's face. It is a healing balm for all that is wrong in this world. I watch, in amazement, as I am discovering who these children are.

I am loved and adored. This is the story of today. I settle into it. I don't wrestle with my identity. I don't wrestle with my purpose. I just live and breathe and use the senses that God has given me to experience this day, moment by moment, and to enjoy this life.

I am alive. I am rich and my heart is full. I am deeply loved. I am present. I have so much to be thankful for.

This is today.

Every Choice Is Too Hard (Where Is the Map for My Life?)
March 14, 2020

Every choice is too hard.

Is there anybody out there who understands what I mean?

I have started down a path for my life, and I honestly have no idea where this is going. I've spent years traveling, hoping to stumble across at least a rudimentary map of what lies ahead. But there isn't one. It has yet to be written. Every turn I take is uncharted territory. I don't know where the story of my life is going to lead me or my family. The mystery of undiscovered lands, the heart-leap of mountain-top views, the deep and dark of forests, the wonder of hidden waterfalls. . . How profoundly will walking through the valleys change us? Are we on the right course? There are so many diverging roads. There are so many choices. So many unknowns. We don't know where we are going to end up. And honestly, sometimes, I am just hoping and praying we are heading in the right direction.

Because I wake up every morning with a million choices in the queue. How we will arrange our lives. . . How much time and energy do I want to put into every aspect of this day?

There are nine of us living in this little house—all needing to be fed, watered, clothed, educated, inspired, nurtured, loved, seen, heard, understood. . . Trying to work this out new every morning can get overwhelming. It is easy to get lost inside a never-ending choose-your-own-adventure story.

I know and truly believe it is a blessing to live an unscripted life, but the simple fact of the matter is: *choices are hard.* Even the easy ones are hard when you are dealing with this many people on a day to day basis. Because what one person needs in any given moment is not the same as what another person needs. And people want plenty that they don't need, myself included. And it is sometimes hard to separate what is essential from what is preferential.

And then there are really hard choices, about things like how many kids we are going to have and if we are going to try to sell our house or if we are thinking about shaking up our plan for family education. And even bigger questions like who are these people anyway and how in this world are we going to raise them to be the souls they were created to be. And this is just normal life! No tragedies, no medical issues, no life-or-death situations. There are so many big questions. There are moments in my everyday reality when it seems as if *everything is at stake.*

And the truth is, there is not a one-size-fits all when it comes to big life choices. And most of the time even the best choices create problems that have to be solved. My children didn't choose to be in a big family. Do I hope and believe that they will be thankful for it? Yes. Does it make their life easier? In some ways, yes. In some ways, no. We have lots of opportunity to work on things like sharing, giving and taking, dealing with different types of personalities. This is a good thing. We also all have to deal with a lot of crying and screaming, a lot of serving people who are younger and less able to help themselves, a whole lot of going *ssslllllllooooooowww*. We have to generally adopt a different pace of life, which, for all its merits, can be a real struggle.

With homeschooling, we are opening a certain kind of window to the world. One where we can create opportunities for learning that traditional school can't. We can give our children time and guidance to pursue their interests. We can allow them the breathing room to go at a different pace. But saying yes to this kind of life is saying no to another. Am I a pro at this? Of course not. Am I am figuring it out as I go? Of course I am. And I am just taking it one day and prayer at a time.

The life journey is difficult, because there are treacherous roads, and there are so many choices that seem good. And so many choices that are good. And yet there is so much to overcome even in the best choices. *And* there is always the unexpected result of a choice made that takes you down a detour and makes you late for what you thought was the real climax of your story. Only to find that the destination no longer exists.

I am just trying to figure out my life, one day at a time. I am just trying to discern which direction to walk. I desperately want a clear path to follow. Someone to hand me a map and say, "Here. This is your life. You will maximize it if you take this road, turn here, cross the river here. Look out for this. Make sure to stop and enjoy the view from this point. . ." But in reality, no one has drawn it out yet. Because I am the first person to walk this specific calling. I was created by God for a unique purpose. And my life *is* the map. And it is still being drawn. I am walking through the human experience, pencil and notebook in hand, writing down the course I have taken. I am looking back over a life of faith, seeing the hand of God in every step of the way. I never thought we would make it this far. I see the unexpected turns we took that once seemed like major detours, and how they actually brought us into land that was fertile and fragrant and full of life. I see valleys where we crossed through the darkest shadows only to come out on the other side where the sun was rising into good green pastures. Deep wells, clear springs, rivers of living water.

My goal in life is to hear from God. I aspire to wake up, lean into him, and pray for vision for this day. (God, show us the things you want to teach us today. Help us to learn what we need to know for our lives today. God, show me how to focus my energy and time today. God, lead me in this next step. Show me where to go and show me how.) Because without him, I can't stress to you enough how I feel the weight of *every single choice*. There are too many unknowns, too many consequences, too many regrets. Too many lives at stake. We are daily standing on the edge of a new landscape. Oh, God, which way do we go?

One thing I have learned from looking back at the map I have scratched out over these last thirty-eight years of my life, and that is this: I refuse to make decisions about where we will go based on fear. I tell you this, trembling. We would have missed *so many blessings* if we had always waited on things to make perfect sense instead of taking a Spirit-led step of faith. God, in his ever-lovingkindness, has always delivered, right on time, everything we need to walk through even our darkest places. And I cannot begin to express to you how lavishly He has done it. He has shown us that He cares profoundly about the details of our lives. I have felt His pleasure again and again as we stood at a crossroad and said *no to fear* and *yes to faith*. He cares about our deep desires. And He continues to take the small seed of faith that we have and turn it into orchards of abundance.

When we walk with Christ, the goal is not to get from point A to point Z on a map that we studied in a textbook. We are living a life that is breaking new ground. In Him, we have access to wonder and surprise, to mercies new every morning, to rivers of life, life more abundant, life everlasting.

Does it mean we never make a misstep? Of course not. But I have seen that even my mistakes can be used by Him, when I offer up a surrendered heart. There is grace upon grace as I give myself over to the purpose He has for my life and the life of my family.

Every choice is too hard. Except for one. Looking back through the pages of my map-journal, I have found only one choice that is always clear. And that is listening for His voice. The only way I know how to live in peace in a world where there are so *many decisions* is by bringing every day before Him, inquiring in every season, and asking Him to lead our family for the glory of His Name. When I listen for his voice, I do not have to worry. I do not have to look back in regret. I just walk by faith, one day at a time. And I believe that God will give me vision to see the next step as He illuminates the way before me.

We are forging a new path. We are clearing a trail for others to see. We are leaving a record of our lives through the ever-expanding spaces that have yet to be seen by human eyes. Our story is a new story, still unfinished. Our journey is a new journey, with lands undiscovered. And my life is the in-progress map of God's grace, mercy, and deliverance.

EMBRACING THIS BREATH

APRIL 9, 2020

The perfect beauty of this morning actually hurts me. As I steal a quiet hour in my little garden with a cup of coffee, the world saturated in green, trees in bloom, birdsong, the first signs of new life coming up in my raised beds. . . My heart aches. The unabashed brilliance of life. It stings. Because there is so much suffering. So many people living in a crisis of one sort or another. So many people asking, with trembling voices, the collective question, "What is going to happen?"

I long for a world where there is no sickness or death, where there are no crises, where there is no corruption or deception, where motives are clear and are for the benefit of humankind.

Where news is good. Where there are no lies. Where there is only truth and only trust. Where there is no evil. Where nature is wild and free but harmless. Where the wolf lays down with the lamb. Where a little child can lead it all.

Jesus, let your Kingdom come.

In the chaos of these past few weeks, I take great comfort in knowing that every day of my life was recorded in God's book before a single day had passed. I know that he put me and my family in this moment in history. We do not know what is going to happen, but God will use all things to work together for the good of those who love Him and are called according to His purpose. I am reminded again that my life is not about my own happiness, my own ambitions, or my own plans. I am reminded that the "security" of my life is not the house I live in, the jobs that pay my bills, or the money I have in the bank. It's not food in the pantry. What felt like the sturdy infrastructure of my life a few weeks ago now seems fragile. Living in this scenario is like holding my breath. I am more aware than ever that there is a greater narrative than the everyday hustle and bustle of existence. That my life is part of a great and overarching story of God's love, grace, and redemption. My life belongs to God. He made me for such a time as this. He put these children in our care for this moment in history. We do not know where we may be asked to go, but we know that He will illuminate the path before us one step at a time. That is all we can ask or hope for—to do his will. To live for his glory. To be a part of His invisible Kingdom that is and is to come.

I refuse to live this sacred moment of my life in fear of what is to come. I embrace the helplessness of my current state. It is a reminder to me that in my weakness, His strength is made perfect. I embrace this season where the structure of my life feels like it could collapse at any moment. It is a reminder to me that I was created by God, and that He is building something out of my life that will stand long after the plagues and destructions and deceptions of this world have come and gone. I was made for life. Abundant. Everlasting. The life we see now is just a shallow breath. I embrace it. Even in such a tenuous moment, life is a sacred gift. I can embrace even this season because God is still in control. So I will not live in fear. Instead, I press myself deeper into the beauty of the day. I see the eyes of those I love—eyes alive with colors as brilliant as any springtime garden. I hear the voices of my husband and children, more beautiful to me than a chorus of birdsong. I lean into the beauty of this moment, praising God for life, for ease of breath, for a morning cup of coffee, for the light of another day. I will face the future with faith and hope and love. And I will teach this to my children. And as long as we have breath, we will praise Him.

THIS MORNING I WAS BORN

This morning I was born. My mother struggled with birth until dawn. I went home in her arms. I cried. I slept. My eyes focused on her beautiful, ephemeral face, familiar somehow though I had never seen it before.

While she was getting pancakes on the table, I bounced on my sister's knee. I listened to the piano. I grabbed a stack of fat crayons and began to scribble on the walls. By the time we sat down to eat, my hair had grown long and brown with thick bangs framing my face. I spilled my orange juice on my pretty dress and went to change into shorts and a t-shirt, put on my backpack, and go to school.

After breakfast, I learned how to read and make letters and numbers. I made a thousand laps around the playground. I made friends and watched them change. I changed. My hair grew longer and my bangs grew out. I filled a dozen journals. I took piano lessons and learned the guitar. I made a few quick trips to the ocean and back. My brothers and sisters went to college and got married. I learned about algebra and chemistry and wars and governments and how to write stories and essays and how to choose words carefully to say exactly what I mean. I was done with high school by noon.

At lunch, time stopped for a split-second when I met the man I would marry. He was carrying a guitar. His voice struck a chord somewhere deep within me. He asked me to sing. We wrote a hundred love songs while we finished up our chocolate cake.

We got married right after lunch, and I spent an hour or so driving back and forth to grad school and work, filling more journals, making music, planning our future. At 1:30, I graduated and we bought a house. I spent the rest of the afternoon having children. 1, 2, 3, 4, 5, 6, 7, 8 times we dropped everything, rushed to the hospital, and I became the mother in another child's story.

Now it is 4:00, and I am just about to have my cup of tea. It is nice to sit down for a few minutes before a busy evening of raising eight children into adulthood, attending their weddings, and babysitting their children. Not to mention dinner prep, clean up, and the books I am hoping to write today.

I honestly don't know how I am going to get it all done before this day is through.

As the steam rises from my cup, I take in the fragrance. I drink the tea down like a shot of hope.

And I linger, for one long, suspended moment-in-time, in the grace that brought me this far.

I STAND IN THIS BREATH
OF MY LIFE

I am alive. I'm trying to let that sink in.

I inherited the unfinished sketchbook of a beloved art professor who passed away last spring. Flipping through the pages this morning, I see how alike we are in our interactions with the blank pages—line drawings, quotation marks surrounding deep theological ideas and questions, to-do lists, ideas scribbled in the singular, everyday handwriting that has become more profound in the absence of the hand. . . Though we were very different people, I see that we processed our worlds in a similar way. We were both enamored by beauty. We searched for it, and recorded our observations in the private worlds of our journals.

But he is gone into the mystery. And I am still here, scribbling away at the meaning of life, sipping tea, raising children, eating, drinking, sleeping, waking to questions that have no answers.

I stand in this breath of my life and look ahead.

And I have hope that makes absolutely no sense. Because the world is full of suffering and heartache, and I will assuredly face things I cannot yet begin to be brave enough to imagine. But I have tasted the goodness of God. I have seen his tender, intimate love and that he is with us in the details of our lives. And so, in spite of loss and pain and suffering, I continue to hope.

I stand in this breath of my life and look behind.

And I give myself grace that I do not deserve. Because I have made mistakes and missteps. I have absolutely failed at so many of the ideals I hold to as a woman, a wife, and a mother. But I have been forgiven, and through the lovingkindness of God, I can look back on my life without regrets.

This is one of the deepest desires of my heart. To breathe. To be fully present, not looking behind in regret or ahead in fear, but to have such trust and faith in God that moment by moment, I am experiencing the riches he extends to me.

HOPE ON THE INHALE

hope
on the inhale
after the gut-punch
the diagnosis, bleak prognosis
look into the mirror
but your eyes can't focus
on any beauty but what's lost

hope
on the inhale
in the breaking of headlines
that beat on the shoreline,
the rising of feartides
that pull you back into despair

hope
on the inhale
after the deep sigh
after the long cry
after the fists-raised-why

hope
on the inhale
after the conversation

the situation
the dissipation of dreams
hearts ripped at the seams

hope
on the inhale
on your face, on your knees
crying, dear God please,
at the bedside of the dying
at the end of all your trying
to understand
how to stand
with the wind
knocked clean out of you

hope
on the inhale
in the ocean waves of sorrow
where the aching, hollow morrow
crashes ceaselessly upon
the shores of today

hope
on the inhale

the broken heart is beating
hope
the weary lungs still breathing
hope
while there is life, there is light
hope
in the darkest night
hope
on the inhale

breathe out fear
and heavy regret
remember my soul
and do not forget
I am sustained by promise
that has not failed me yet

hope
on the inhale

though my way may lead
through perilous lands
I rest in the miracles
of unseen hands
and live and breathe
and have my being

in Christ, eternal hope
hope in the future
hope in the past
hope in this moment
where life can be lived
fully, without fear and
without regret
hope, hope, hope

on every inhale

hope

QUESTIONS AT 2 A.M.

THE SPACE BETWEEN
HERE AND A MIRACLE
MARCH 7, 2020

If you are up, like me, at 2 a.m., wrestling with questions that do not seem to have answers, tired of trying to drown out your own thoughts so you can finally get some sleep, welcome to my kitchen table. I just got here myself, made a pot of tea, grabbed my Bible, a journal, and a pencil. I am hoping for about two hours before the baby wakes again. . . So take a breath, sit with me, relax, grab a mug, and let's talk it over.

Life is hard. It sometimes feels like those bad dreams where you show up to take a math test and realize that you have skipped so many classes you have no idea what in the world the test is even about. Isn't it hard enough to just figure out *you*? Throw a husband and a handful of children into the equation, and you've got an exam with way too many questions that you are desperately hoping turns out to be multiple choice.

Sometimes, I feel like I am squeezed into a tiny corner of my own life, without the kinds of choices I really want to make. I am limited by my own resources or my energy levels or by the consequences of choices I have already made. I feel like I need breathing room. I need a quiet place to go and think. I need to figure it out. Because there are just so many things that aren't working.

I am staring into a brick wall. And it will not budge. And I can't see what is on the other side. But I know I need to get there. I am literally six inches away from seeing these prayers that I have poured into journal after journal, day after day, week after week, year after year, *answered*. But when? And how? And why do I have to wait so long to see this hope fulfilled? Will I ever even see what is on the other side of this massive wall?

I am asking these questions in the 2 a.m. kitchen, because there is not another time I can hear my own thoughts clearly enough to articulate them. Life just doesn't slow down. Ever.

Where is this all going, God? How useful can my life be when I am constantly trying to figure out how to make every single day work for us?

I wait. I breathe. I sip my tea. I feel something like hope start to rise up like a bird as a phrase forms in my mind. I scratch it down in my journal before it flies away.

I want to tell it to you. Because you are up with me. Maybe it will mean something to you, too.

You are standing in the space between here and a miracle.

I am letting it sink in.

I want to get on the other side of this wall. I want to know the answer to this question. I want to see the future. I want to know how to make plans. I want to know that all of my children are going to be ok. That they will have everything they need. That they will be planted in the garden where they can flourish. I want to know how to do this high level math that I somehow never studied. I want to know that we are doing what we were created to do. I want to see doors open wide that we are meant to walk through.

But right now, I am standing in front of a great wall.

I am standing in the space between here and a miracle.

There is no way that I can climb it or go around it or go through it. I have tried everything.

I have come to the end of my own thoughts, ideas, and resources. And that is a good place to be. *Because that is the space between here and a miracle.*

In life, anything can happen. There is always hope. There are always miracles, great and small. Yes, the wall is real and solid and I am standing on what feels like the wrong side of it. But look at all the beauty on this side, even in the little corner of my own life. The miracle of the eye that reflects light back to my brain and allows me to read these words. The miracle of flowering trees and the color and fragrance of a robust black tea. The miracle of finding a quiet time to sit at this kitchen table and have this conversation with you. The miracle of motherhood, of children moving through my body and being born into the world. The miracle of laughter. The miracle of finding out I didn't really need what I thought I couldn't live without. The miracle of friendship and resources that spring up from unexpected places. The miracle of light. The miracle of belonging to God, who owns everything and knows every answer to every question and discerns our deepest needs. This is the great expanse on which we build our lives. That every trial, every question, every restless night has meaning and purpose. And that when there is no way forward, a life that is fully surrendered to the will of God continues to trust Him. Because this is faith—the substance of things hoped for, the evidence of things not seen.

This is how we walk through life—by faith, not by sight.

Tonight, it doesn't matter what is on the other side of that wall. I may be looking at something that is currently impassible, but look behind me. I have come so far, by miraculous grace and everlasting mercy. And this wall is not the end of my story. I am living in the great expanse of a life that is surrendered to God. There is no possibility that is beyond his calling. I can go back to bed and sleep in peace. Because I am resting in the space between here and a miracle.

ON WORDS
(IN EVERY STORM, MERCY)
APRIL 5, 2019

Words are a comfort to me. They press in around me while I am lying awake in bed. I can feel the word *mercy* wrap me up like a weighted blanket. I have heard the heavy clank and felt the ground shake under the weight of that word as it anchored my soul to the bottom of a raging ocean. It held me there until a great storm had passed.

I hold onto words like *hope* the way I wrap my arms around my two-year-old daughter, who journeys down the long, dark staircase every night around midnight to find me. I squeeze that word in close and breathe in the fragrance of it. And I feel the warmth and glow that surrounds it. I go to sleep with its light pressed against my heart.

Momentum is a word that keeps knocking on my front door. I shut the door quickly, because I have too much laundry, too many house projects, too many people on my mind to sit and chat with her about how the baby will be here in six weeks and I have yet to look in the attic and see if I still have newborn clothes. I know what is going to happen. I will be in the middle of a regular day of schooling, dishes, read-alouds, rearranging, trying to savor life, and I'll stop with a sudden

153

jerk and realize I'm in labor. And that will start a new momentum that will change the history of the world. But I don't have time to discuss this with her. So I block her calls and send her letters back, unopened.

Some words I have to chase away in dreams. I bat them off with pillows. Words like *time*—which never seems to be moving at the right speed. It is always trying to sweep me up too fast and carry me too high above the ground—on balloons or kites or in the clutches of a great bird of prey. . . Or it is begging me to let everything else go and just sit with it, bask in it, ask for more of the golden sunshine of it. I am spending it too fast. I am not making the most of it. I am going to lose the precious bit of it I have. God forbid, I am wasting it. Or I am going to run out of it.

The word *comfort* sits with me. She sings to me like my mother did when I was a child. My beautiful mother by moonlight. She strokes my hair and tells me to think of happy things when I have a bad dream that is actually not a dream at all but something that could very well really happen. Or something that is happening right now. She tells me that I am loved, that my life has meaning, that there is no need to be afraid. I believe her. And under the influence of her lilting voice, I finally drift off to sleep.

It is seasons like the one I am now living that I am grateful for these marks that represent letters that combine to make words that ignite thought and can carry me through the unrelenting momentum of time passing with the hope and comfort of God's unending mercy.

LOOKING DEEPLY INSIDE MYSELF

MAY 28, 2020

5:17 a.m. My eyes open in bed. I had a dream that woke first my mind, then my body. My face is pressed against a sweet, softly-sleeping baby. In the dark I lift him up and carry him across the room to place him gently in his crib. He doesn't wake. A small miracle.

I walk back over to my bed, stepping over baskets of yesterday's laundry. I check the time. 5:19. While still in motion, for a split-second, I think about my soft pillow, and how without the baby I will be able to sleep in any position I want. But before I can even sit on the edge of the bed to decide if I am going to get up or go back to sleep, I make my move. My sleepy, unsuspecting body follows as I grab my sweater and my glasses and walk into the kitchen, pour water into the kettle, and open up my journal.

I write.

I write about being sleepy and the fragrance of tea. I write about the dream of my beautiful mother and the ache I still feel when I wake and remember she is gone. I write about the baby, whose life is a balm to my soul. I write about the early wren who is singing in the dark and how that surely means something. I write a list of all the things I need to do today, knowing that not even half will get done. I write about my children. Their musical voices, their explosive creativity, their unquenchable thirst to learn. Their strengths and weaknesses. My strengths and weaknesses. The way Heidi looked in her beautiful blue dress, her bright eyes shining and her auburn hair softly shimmering in the sunshine. How that image in my mind represents a depth of feeling I can never say in words. How I hope I am doing this right. How raising these souls is such a one-shot deal. How they are growing up right before my eyes. I write a prayer that God will give me vision. That He will show me how to meet these needs that rise up, one by one, like ocean waves. That I will not drown in them. But that He will give me love and joy and peace and patience and kindness and goodness and gentleness and faithfulness and self-control by the power of His Spirit which lives within me. I write about how utterly helpless I am without Him.

I write about the last of the bleeding hearts, strung out like beads on the vine in my Daddy's garden. I would wear them around my neck if they would last. And about the way water pools in perfect, crystal-pearls in the center of the nasturtium leaves. And how I hope today will be the first day I see their jeweled blooms. I write the details of my life, which feel so much more significant when they are put on paper.

6:10 a.m. I am wide awake. In the pages of this blank book, I learn what I think and feel. I read the words as I write them. And I am often surprised by what I find when I read my story. The simple practice of showing up and writing my thoughts, day after day in every season, has transformed my life like nothing else. As I force thoughts into words, which move through my brain into my arm and shake out of the ink in this pen onto the page, I learn who I am. I look at these words on the paper. I search them out like someone looking for buried treasure. Surely there is something of value that can be mined up from the vast landscape of my life.

The house is beginning to stir. It is almost time to put all these thoughts away and get focused on the needs that will rise to meet me all day long. But at 6:47 a.m., I am facing them head-on. Through the act of showing up, writing down my thoughts and offering them up to God, I am yielding my life to His purpose for me. I have prayed for vision, and I know that every small ritual of my existence is bound up in that. I can give myself more fully to the day because my life means something. I can give myself more fully to others because I have looked deeply inside myself and I know that I am part of a story.

It is a story I am living, reading, and writing at the same time.

THE SLEEPING FACE OF MY BEAUTIFUL BOY

After the lullaby, I see the sleeping face of my beautiful boy, two years old. And at once, all the world is still. Time moves forth from this moment in reluctant ripples. Slow-moving reflections of memories, past and future that will become a whole life. Separate from my own, but always flowing in and out and leading to the same ocean.

I well up with gratitude that he is my child and he is in this world. And in the same breath, I grieve that this world is full of things that will threaten the very peace that now gently animates his whole being. I imagine all the possibilities of his life, impressions sweet and tender, terrible and tremulous.

Fear would like to choke all of my most beautiful dreams. It would like to take the wondrous joy out of even this moment, where loveliness emanates like a lighted candle in a dark room.

But as I look at the face that wakes my heart to longing, to a knowing that life itself is the most precious gift ever given me, I take heart. And I turn my whole being to the God who creates and sustains all of it. He has not left us defenseless, eyes closed, blindly groping for a way forward. Even in darkness, he has given us dreams and vision. He has given us Himself, and he has given us eternity. And the terrors of this world are shadows that are dispelled by the everlasting light of his presence.

I make a memory of this sleeping face. For the beauty of it. And for the image that I want to settle into my soul. Oh my soul, rest. Be at peace.

The Lord your God is with you, he is mighty to save. He will take great delight in you, he will quiet you with his love, he will rejoice over you with singing. (Zephaniah 3:17 NIV)

LIVING WITH VISION
FEBRUARY 27, 2019

I am up early this morning, before the little ones. In my closet-office (where I sit in a corner at a small desk, typing this under a rack of hanging clothes), I am armed with a steaming mug of Darjeeling tea, a muffin, and the promise of a glorious uninterrupted hour of writing and thinking and praying (thanks to my eleven-year-old daughter, who woke early with me and is drinking her own cup of tea in the kitchen, on call for me if the babies wake). The quiet of this moment is such a luxury. It is the only time I have to process what is happening in my life. Where we have been, where we are headed. What it all means.

Any moment, this house will start to wake. By breakfast time, the clatter and clamor of questions will overtake me. Food on the table, conversation, spilling drinks, refilling drinks, clearing the table, memory work, violin practice, piano practice, ukulele practice, math, reading, throwing in a load of laundry, picking up the toys, dishwasher, managing schedules, lunchtime, clean-up, quiet time, piano lessons, throwing in another load of laundry, dinner, conversation, spilling drinks, refilling drinks, clearing the table, dishes, sweeping, toys, vacuum, all the little rows of teeth, diapers, bedtime, bedtime, bedtime. . .

Life is such a blur.

It is so easy to lose sight of what this is all about and to just drown in the relentlessness of these needs that hit me, one by one, minute by minute, day after restless night and day.

In the stillness of this morning, I am seeing clearly. There is something that I need every day of my life. Before my eyes ever open. More than tea. More than food. More than a few moments of peace and quiet. I need it as desperately as I need the air I am breathing.

Vision.

I have prayed for vision all my life. I needed it when I was young. When I was standing on the edge of girlhood and womanhood, when I was looking into the future, imagining myself living with the man I now call my husband. When I thought of us building our lives together, I prayed for vision. I didn't really know for sure if we were meant to be together. But I thought we were, and God gave me just enough faith to say yes to forever.

Fast forward fifteen years. We are expecting our seventh child in May. God, if I have ever needed vision in my life, I need it now. Not only vision for myself, but for each of these fearful, wonderful, unique-in-this-world souls that share life with us. I need it for making the days run smoothly in a home where eight (soon to be nine) people wake and learn and eat and grow and have needs and desires and ambitions great and small. I need vision for keeping some kind of order in this house, for homeschool, for understanding my own purpose in the midst of motherhood, for surrendering more profoundly to marriage and the gifts and struggles it brings, for tempering and channeling all of the creative ideas that spill out the windows and doors of this little house. For cultivating the beauty you have planted in each of these little hearts. Oh, God, I need vision.

I need vision to see that the mundane rituals of motherhood are infused with rich, deep meaning. Stacks of dishes are a symbol of a sacred gathering around the table, where we are looking into one another's eyes, enjoying a meal, and sharing the conversation that is shaping our lives. Mountains of laundry are a symbol of life that is lived in every color of the rainbow. The evidence that we have had the joy of play, of getting dirty, of experiencing life with children. And that a life with children is a life with wonder.

I need vision to see that homeschool is not just about a standard, textbook education. But that God has created each one of these little people in my care to impact the Kingdom. That each life has a purpose greater than I can now comprehend. That their lives will touch other lives. And that the subjects of kindness, compassion, forgiveness, are as important as reading, writing, and arithmetic. I need vision to clue me in to who these children are becoming, how they are wired, how to lay down a broad foundation for learning and eventually help them to narrow the focus down to where their purpose and passions lie. I need vision to keep a flexible plan in place for learning and experiencing life.

I need vision to meet the ever-changing needs of these children. To see them as God sees them. To love them through their struggles. To make life work in every season. I need vision to create the barest of routines that we can plug our lives into. To be disciplined enough to help all of these people to follow through day by day with a well prayed-out plan. And I need vision to see when this routine is no longer working, to get down on my knees and cry out to God for a new idea that will carry us through the next season of life.

Being a mother is teaching me that vision is crucial to finding purpose in everyday life. It is how we find our way. Living with vision is living in collaboration with God. And living in collaboration with God is where we find the intersection of the sacred and the everyday.

KEEPING PART OF YOU ALIVE
(MOTHERHOOD AND THE CREATIVE LIFE)

Sometimes I look in the mirror and barely recognize myself. What happened to that person I used to be—the one who was bubbling over with good ideas and introduced to strangers with an impressive trail of accomplishments following her name? The person who had dreams and ambitions greater than getting every room in the house clean at the same time. She was the one I was counting on to organize my life, to write my book, to check off all the goals on my daily, weekly, monthly, yearly, and lifelong to-do lists. She was the one I was hoping would do something worthwhile with this breath of earthly existence I call my life.

But she can be really hard to get in touch with.

I am thirty-nine years old. I am a mother of small children. What once seemed like the central vision for my life has slowly moved out of sight and into the rearview mirror. I know that I am meant to be a mother. I never doubt that. I know that I am blessed beyond measure to have eight healthy, beautiful children who keep my life full of wonder. I know that one day I will miss these very busy days, and I will look back in disbelief at how I ever thought it a chore to tuck the babies into their little beds at night and see them through till they fell asleep.

But. . .

Raising young children and meeting needs sun-up to sun-down (and usually through the night) is exhausting. Beautiful, yes. But exhausting. I often feel there is little time and/or energy for anything that is not directly related to caring for these little ones. And out of necessity, I have let a lot of things that I thought were an essential part of who I am fall away.

But there is a seed of vision that has wanted to continue living and growing. It would like to flourish. It would like to be a whole garden, but there is no time in this season of short daylight hours for cultivating something so labor-intensive as that. It reaches up for sunlight in the early morning, before the babies wake, before the day is crowded with the colorful voices of this home. The little tree grows, season by season, sometimes flowering, sometimes lying dormant. But it wants to live. Despite my neglect, despite my occasional whim to uproot it altogether and throw it into the compost of my life, this little tree continues to grow, and at times, it flourishes.

And for this, I am thankful.

Sometimes, as mothers, there are seasons where there is so little time to cultivate creative vision that the best we can do is commit to keeping that part of us alive as we lovingly turn our hearts to the needs of our children. They are our world. They are our focus. And though we are holding onto this thread of who we are, we are allowing motherhood to work on us as part of the creative process. Of course, our children are changing us. We wouldn't want it any other way. They wake us up to beauty (the moon, a firefly, a perfectly-ripe summer peach). They fill us up with laughter. They deepen every one of our emotions. They draw us closer to one another. They teach us to love and forgive. They force us to get up out of bed when life deals us a difficult blow. They truly gift us with the ability to strip it down to the essentials. To let go of so many things that are not serving us. And to conserve our energy for what really is important.

But there is something inside of us, separate from our children, at the core of who we are, that we need to hang onto. It is the one little seed of purpose that was planted before these little people were born. And cultivating this little tree will bring great fruit into the life of our family.

For me, it is writing. That is pretty much the only thing that can get me—by my own will—out of bed at 5:30 a.m. on a morning like this. I used to do a lot of other things. But I have found that creatively, I am satisfied when I write. I write in journals daily, and I keep a list of ideas with me at all times in case inspiration strikes. I am constantly coming back to my book or to my blog, incorporating the details of my life into the story. And even though I don't write as much as I'd like, and even though I don't finish *anything* as quickly as I feel I should, over time, I am making significant progress toward something that feels connected to the reason I was put on this earth. Writing helps me understand my life. It helps me process the world around me, which, despite its aching beauty—let's face it—is often chaotic and messy. I write because it makes me feel alive. It wakes me up to the miracle of my life as a mother and a woman and a human traveling through this world. It is a mirror for my soul. It is my most genuine prayer. It is the little tree that I am trying to keep alive in every season. And ultimately, taking a few minutes every day to do the thing that makes me feel authentically *me* allows me to give myself over more fully to the needs and desires of my family. I recognize that when I have found time to cultivate this vision, I am a better mother. And I am more able to help these children see and tend to their own incredible and creative voices.

POEM AT 2 A.M.

Oh the fragility
of earthly life,
an unrehearsed song
achingly sweet,
carried on the winds
of a broken world
on butterfly wings.

Oh my soul
wake up, and live
and sing out loud.
The song of the spirit
is a candle
that cannot be put out.
It is a poem
made of brilliant light,
a recitation
to be spoken
in the middle
of the darkest night.

FAITH AND MIRACLES

ARE YOU GOING TO HAVE MORE?

People are always asking me if we are going to have more children. The tiniest bit of small talk can tease this question out of a complete and utter stranger. We go from eye contact, to a silent headcount of my eight kids, to *are all these yours* and *are you going to have more?*

We never even make it to the weather. We skip over it completely because apparently my family planning is even more of a mundane subject.

There are lots of short answers to this question. Sweet answers, funny answers, turn-it-back-around and see-how-you-like-it answers. The way I respond depends on the day and the way in which the original question is asked.

I have often wondered why people are so curious and think it is because when they ask if I am going to have more children, there is another truer, deeper question that is never posed but always implied:

Why?

In this passage, I would like to share my real, honest-to-God, heartfelt answer to this question. Because it is frustrating to only be able to give short answers to something so incredibly profound as the choice to bring a living soul into the world. And nobody in the cereal aisle really wants to stand there long enough for me to share my story.

But I would like to share it with you.

I never planned on being a mother. I didn't plan on *not* being a mother. I didn't think about it. I never planned on having a large family. I didn't plan on having *any* family. I fell in love. Deep water. I wanted to be with this man for the rest of my life, which I naively imagined would be all about us and how we would add our creative mark on the world. We knew we would likely have a family one day. And while I imagined parenting would be a beautiful, sacred experience, I considered it secondary to the real mission of my life.

And then we started having children. And slowly, the vision for my life started changing. Because motherhood has changed me from the inside out.

I never set out to have a big family. I have wanted to run away from this quiet and gentle calling that I've felt on my life many times. I have wanted to be done. I don't know how many times I have said *I can never do this again*. . . But each time, I have felt a pull in my heart to open the door for one more

173

child to walk through. And here we are, 15 years into parenting, with eight beautiful souls that live with us and are forever a part of us. I never had the faith to say I am going to have eight children. But God didn't require that of me. He gave me the faith to say yes to one more, eight times.

Once I saw a woman with 14 children. They were all ages and sizes—babies and beautiful girls and young women and women, and they all looked alike. The older girls were holding and caring for the younger ones. I cried. It moved me.

I once watched a performance of a family of 12 playing bluegrass music. Their harmonies were what only family harmonies can be. And I wept like a baby.

Childbirth is a road I have walked nine times in 15 years. Down this path, I have encountered and faced the deepest and darkest fears of my life. I have wrestled with the fear of the unknown, the fear of pain, the fear of dying. I have begun to overcome fear with faith, one sacred birth at a time. I have experienced one of the greatest sorrows of my life on this road, watching helplessly as the little one we had all begun to picture as a part of our family began to slip away into the darkness. I have felt the bitter-cold gusts of grief blow right through me at the thought of the little life I will always miss and carry in my heart. And my hope in heaven has grown stronger because of the treasure I have waiting there.

Through childbirth, I have encountered the purest form of joy. The unspeakable kind. The kind that fills you up to overflowing. Going to the edge of the world, coming so close to the limits of what a human body can do, and coming back with a beautiful, pink, perfect baby and just sitting there, laughing, not believing it is over and you won the prize.

When I look back over these years of having children, I think of how many times we have wrestled with the decision to let our family grow or keep it as it is. I remember times my husband said, "Let's always have a baby in the house. . ." or "I feel richer having children than anything else I could have in life." How we said we were overwhelmed and exhausted and didn't think we could handle more. How we never had money and we didn't know how we would provide for the children we had, much less any more that might be born in the future. How I went in for pre-op to have my tubes tied and could not go through with it because I had a vision of the inexplicable joy I would feel if I looked upon the face of the baby we almost didn't have. A baby that has since been born. A baby with a face and fingers and a voice. A baby who brought peace and joy and life into our chaos. A baby who could calm anybody in this family down with one look of her perfect chubby face. A baby who is dearly loved, and her two little brothers that followed right behind her. How close we came to never knowing them. The profound mystery of it takes my breath away.

These little ones are not just babies. They are human souls that have eternal purpose in the world and in the world to come. I tremble when I think about it. They aren't just children. They are learners and thinkers, they are musicians and artists, they are builders and dreamers, they are friends and teachers, they are writers and scholars, they are husbands and wives and fathers and mothers, they are soul and spirit. Their presence in this world changes it forever.

And we love them. And we like them. And we couldn't imagine our lives without *any one* of them.

I consider being open to having another child part of God's calling and purpose and blessing for my life in this season. How long will this season last? I don't know. Do I have to know?

No. Because God is gracious to allow life to unfold before us. All imaginations of our future are short-sighted and based in a reality that will cease to exist. Life is incredibly complex. I don't know my own future. I don't know what will happen in the years to come to change my perspective. All I can do is seek God's will for my life in this day and in this moment, trusting He will continue to show me the way. And that is what I'm trying to do.

So are we going to have more?

We will have to wait and see.

HELPLESS

Helpless. The word rose up out of my mind and offered itself to me in the middle of a dark night. I held a feverish child in my arms, watched his labored breathing, imagined the flickering candle of his precious little life before my eyes. My mind traveled farther than I meant it to go, and left me considering my own mortality and the mortality of these beautiful ones who have been so lovingly stitched into the most secret places of my heart.

Even in the time-suspended, wide-eyed-panic of the moment, I knew the word was a lie. I knew that in life and death, in sickness and health, in understanding and mystery, I was held in the hands of God. That there is life beyond life. That there is no separating what God has joined together. I didn't feel it. But I knew it.

I lift up my eyes to the hills, from whence comes my help. My help comes from the Lord, the Maker of heaven and earth. (Psalm 121:1-2)

Faith wants to be big enough to say yes to anything God would ask of me. It pushes me up against the hardest places and searches for an opening that I can move through. But sometimes, faith isn't big enough to walk through walls. It can only say, with trembling hands:

God, you have to show me what to do next.

And he does. And you do it. And the dawn breaks. And you move into a new day, different.

In the night, the waves crash loudly against the shore. The sea goes on forever, the brokenness of man echoed over and over in the deep, mournful song it sings.

Faith wants to be big enough to say yes to anything God would ask of me. It pushes me under, wave by wave, searching for a tide that can lift me up onto my feet. But sometimes, faith isn't big enough to walk on water. It can only say with trembling heart:

God, you have to show me what to do next.

And he does. And you do it. And the dawn breaks. And you move into a new day, different.

I lift up my eyes to the hills, from whence comes my help. My help comes from the Lord, the Maker of heaven and earth.

Life is hard. We are living in a broken world where it sometimes feels too risky to love deeply. There is so much to lose.

When my faith trembles, when fear would threaten my total paralysis and regret would strike me deaf and dumb, I wrap myself up in the tender words of Christ. "Whoever desires to come after Me, let him deny himself, and take up his cross, and follow Me. For whoever desires to save his life will lose it, but whoever loses his life for My sake and the gospel's will save it. For what will it profit a man if he gains the whole world, and loses his own soul?" (*Matthew 16:24-26*) And I remind myself that everything I truly have is eternally secure. In life, I have already lost it all. I have already given my life over to Christ, who is in control and *assumes all risk*. I am not meant to carry the weight of the world. I am simply walking, hand in hand, with my Savior. Without fear, without regret, with gratitude and one sincere prayer always upon my lips:

God, please show me what to do next.

And he does. And I do it. And the dawn breaks into the day where his mercies are ever-new. And I live and breathe and have my being in the One who is making this broken world right.

I will lift up my eyes to the hills—
From whence comes my help?
My help comes from the Lord,
Who made heaven and earth.
He will not allow your foot to be moved;
He who keeps you will not slumber.
Behold, He who keeps Israel
Shall neither slumber nor sleep.
The Lord is your keeper;
The Lord is your shade at your right hand.

The sun shall not strike you by day
Nor the moon by night.
The Lord shall preserve you from all evil;
He shall preserve your soul.
The Lord shall preserve your going out and your coming in
From this time forth, and even forevermore.
(from Psalm 121 NKJV)

MY HEART TREMBLES AND SINGS

my own dear child

eyes of bluest bright, alight

body in holy motion

brimming over with lifesong

and the beating, beating, beating heart

beautiful breath

that flows inside you

like a melody

for the gift of your love

and living presence

my heart trembles

and sings

HOW DO YOU FEED THEM?
JUNE 16, 2020

One of the first questions people ask me when I tell them we have seven children is, "How do you feed them?"

It's posed as a joke, and even though I've been asked this dozens of times, I still scramble for a good response. I know people don't only mean how do we pay for food, but also implied is how do we even *do it*? Financially, physically, emotionally. . . It seems like so much. So exhausting. So overwhelming. Why would we choose this life? And now that we've chosen it, how does it actually work? I don't have time to say what I'd really like to say when someone asks me this in line at the grocery store. But I have time to tell you now. So I am going to give you the most honest answer I can.

How do we feed them?

We feed them out of the abundance of God's grace and miracles.

Let me explain. Yes, we work hard. We have a few part-time jobs that we combine to make a living, but the truth is there have been many seasons in our family where we have lived on a steady diet of God's goodness, his faithfulness, and his quiet miracles. We seek him, we ask him for wisdom, we ask him to lead our family. We pray for vision, and over and over again, we have felt him leading us to remain open to having another child. As crazy as it seems. Even in times when the cupboards were bare. He has always shown us that when we seek his will for our lives, and when we step out in faith and obedience, He will provide everything we need.

Looking back over *just this year*, I have been amazed at all of the tender ways God has revealed his love for us. My heart is just overflowing with his goodness. And because of this, I want to share with you seven stories of quiet miracles that our family has seen since January of 2020.

Here we go.

I began the year feeling, again, that we could not live in this house another season. I re-began my inexhaustible search to find the right house. I did all the research, consulted a realtor-friend, had all my friends praying, spent half my waking hours poring over new listings. I felt desperate that this family of nine could not spend another year in this little house on this little piece of land in such an unstable, crazy world. I felt the need to be more self-sufficient. Well-water, good soil, space for chickens or goats should we ever need them, space for my children to roam and explore. . . When I visited a farmhouse with acres and acres of beautiful open space, my eyes welled up with tears. This was where I imagined raising my family. But all the doors were closed.

At some point, it became obvious that apart from a miracle, we would be staying in this house indefinitely. We don't want more debt. That is the opposite of beautiful, open, expansion. And nothing we could afford was better than what we already had. So, I flipped that restless switch in my heart and decided to make the best of what we had.

And here begin the miracles of our year...

Our church was going to be remodeling their kitchen, and our family was offered the old cabinets and counters if we wanted them. At first we hesitated because we couldn't envision where they might go. We had considered putting a kitchenette in our in-progress basement. So, we decided to go ahead and say yes. They were delivered to our basement door, and over the course of several weeks of rearranging, we ended up creating a kitchenette (still to be plumbed!), a huge workspace with counters and cabinets in Randy's basement shop-room, and two walls of overhanging cabinets in our laundry room. The cabinets fit perfectly into these spaces and literally look like they were built for our house. We reorganized our things and gained more space. *Miracle #1—The Cabinet Miracle.*

The basement was very cold last winter. (This was our first year of using the basement as actual house-space. Through a series of barter transactions—teaching music lessons for labor—we poured a concrete floor, did a bit of electric work, and built walls for a storage/utility closet, Randy's shop, and a future bathroom.) We had some money in savings for house projects, but it was running low. We decided that a top priority would be a wood-burning stove or a ventless gas fireplace, although we seriously doubted that we had the money in our budget to purchase and install either. I was overwhelmed by all the research involved. Which would be the better system for heating? Which would be the most cost-effective in the long-run? Which would be the easiest to maintain and keep our children safe? We finally decided that we would look into the gas fireplace and had a date planned on Thursday to go do some in-person research. Over the weekend, our dryer died. Another unexpected expense. . . On Tuesday, Randy got a message from his friend, Eddie. Eddie asked if Randy was still interested in his keyboards, which he was selling at an amazing price. (Earlier in the year we had discussed the possibility of purchasing them.) Randy explained in his message that we didn't have the money because we had to buy a dryer and that we really needed to use the money on a ventless gas fireplace if we could even afford it yet. Eddie wrote back immediately and said, "You have to call me right now."

And here is the second miracle. Randy called Eddie, who had cancer and had been very sick. Eddie said that the same morning, a friend of his had called and said he had been thinking about him and wanted to stop by. When he came, he said he wanted to bless him, and he gave him a dryer and a ventless gas fireplace. Eddie said, "Thanks, man. I don't need these right now, but I'll put them in my garage until I figure out what to do with them." The same morning!!! Eddie delivered them both to our house the next day. The fireplace heats our basement in about 5 minutes. We were able to buy the keyboards, which blessed both Eddie and us, and still have money in our house fund. And we were given the dryer and the fireplace as gifts. I call this *The Fire/Dryer Miracle.* Miracle #2.

I woke up one morning wanting to plant a garden. I called my Daddy, who is an incredible artist in the garden. He was driving when I called, so he pulled over to talk to me. I asked him what I could plant that wouldn't die. He said, "Mack, your problem is your soil. What you really need is some good topsoil." He also told me that he hadn't seen any good topsoil in years. Then he paused and asked me to wait a minute, that he would call right back. A few minutes later, the phone rang and he told me that in the parking lot where he had pulled over, a man was shoveling topsoil. He asked him if he could buy some, and the man agreed to sell Daddy a dump-truck full. That afternoon, he came and unloaded a truckload full of glorious earth into my backyard. My first real garden. I have already enjoyed radishes, arugula, and kale, and I am just seeing the first tiny tomatoes and zucchini flowers. Gardening is another miracle all together. *But my garden is my own quiet, personal miracle.* Miracle #3.

A friend is moving this summer, and she is going through all of her things. She is a little older than me, and her youngest child is older than my first. She and I share a similar philosophy about life and creativity, homeschool, living with vision and purpose, and allowing children to explore and create and read great books. So she began bringing me things. It started with boxes of books—homeschool curriculum that seemed custom-built for my children. Then came the bookshelves and a box or two of art supplies. And then the downpour. Have you ever been to someone's house who has been gardening for a lifetime? Where you realize no one just makes a garden like this happen in a few years? And you just stand in awe. (This is how I feel in my Daddy's garden.) Well, my friend Michelle eventually passed on to me what felt like a life-garden of books, art supplies, games, and toys. All things that inspire creative play and learning. Any craft I had ever wanted to dabble in, I now own a starter set of the materials. I am talking about twenty or thirty big boxes of amazing supplies. A life-garden for my children to play in. This was the fourth miracle. *The Homeschool Mama Soul-Friend Moving Miracle.* And what was equally amazing was the fact that I had empty cabinets waiting to hold these treasures when they arrived.

I have entertained the idea of beekeeping for several years. I thought it might be something we would do one day when we move to the country. Maybe inspired by my garden, I woke one morning and declared, at the breakfast table, that I was going to talk to my beekeeper friend, Joel, and find out what the initial investment of time and money would be to start keeping bees. Randy was hesitant, but said I should look into it. I made the call, got an initial understanding that yes, it was an investment in both time and money, but that it was doable. I asked Randy what he thought about it. He said he didn't feel like it was something we should do right now. I said ok. I truly wasn't pushing. I just had that bit of intuition about it, but wasn't sure if it was a path we should pursue or a desire that would be fulfilled in another season. I really wasn't even sure if bees would be happy in our yard, where the best thing we have to offer them is the dandelions that grow in our lawn. I let it go.

A few days later, I was standing in the front yard and saw a commotion over in the corner. A small swarm of honeybees were building comb inside my water meter! I went in to get Randy. He came out, took one look, and said, "Honey, if God is giving us the bees, I am not going to say no. . ." And that began the story of our beekeeping adventure. We had to save them, because the city policy is to spray and kill them. So Joel came and helped us move them into a bee box. And day one as my life as a beekeeper, I got to taste the honey. And so did Randy and our children. And he became sold on the idea. I literally barely know what I am doing. But I have a stack of books and a friend who is helping me. And they are our bees. They chose us. As humble a home as we have, they wanted to live with us. And this is the fifth miracle. *The Sweet Miracle of My Honeybees.*

The sixth miracle I want to share with you is *The Hidden Room Miracle.* I have been writing and developing an online course about journaling. This means so much to me, and I have realized suddenly that I have something to share that I know backwards and forwards and could talk about all day long. I have been logging countless hours on this work, but I really haven't had space in my house to work without interruption. Earlier in the year, I turned my closet-office into a closet-nursery, giving the baby crib the space that used to house my desk. This was a small miracle of its own, with the baby sleeping right inside our room, but with a bit more privacy. I have, however, missed my own little space. I've been leaving the house for whole days at a time, working wherever I can find quiet. (My Daddy's garden, a local camp that has been vacant this summer. . .) But two weeks ago, it hit me that I need to find a space of my own in this house. I went to bed and woke up knowing exactly what I was going to do. The next week, I spent every spare minute rearranging literally every room of the house to make it work, and I transformed our utility/storage closet into an office for myself. Complete with a door that locks and enough space for a writing desk, a bookshelf for all of my journals, another bookshelf for books, a huge storage shelf for my personal favorite art/craft supplies, a small table for an electric tea kettle, a teapot, and my favorite mug. Did I mention the door locks? I can leave out my stuff. I can work any time of the night or day when I can get away. This is a huge miracle.

I will leave you with one more. I was having a quiet conversation with a friend in my office last week. She is a homeschooling mother of six children. Her oldest children are grown, and she has a beautiful, calm, peaceful quality about her that ministers to me deeply. I was telling her about this season of my life—how full of blessing it is, how much my oldest children are helping me. That so much of parenting in the early years is learning to die to yourself, and that I am relieved to be in a new season where I feel like God is giving me a little bit of myself back. And that my children are helping to bring it out of me. She smiled and said, "Don't you think that is interesting? You now have seven children, more than you have ever had before, and I hear you saying that it is easier than it has ever been." She said that many people don't understand this dynamic, but it is true. And I realized that it is such a miracle. This new season where I have such amazing helpers. My children, who know me and love me and want the best for me, as I know and love and want the best for them. *This is the Surprising Miracle of My Growing Children.*

There have been other miracles. Beautiful, glorious boxes full of groceries delivered by friends who know all our favorite foods, a friend who came and pressure-washed our house as a gift to us, unexpected money in the mail sent at just the right moment to meet a need, the miracle of conversations that came at just the right time to help us make an important decision. . . I could go on and on. This is how we live. This is the life that our children experience, and they can trace the hand of God providing every need throughout their entire lives. They are being raised on God's goodness. They are being brought up on a legacy of seeing how He meets our needs and cares for them as he cares for the sparrows and the lilies of the field.

I am writing this because I want to share God's faithfulness. And because I truly want to remember this year. We are living in the lovingkindness of God. I say this with trembling and reverence and joy and peace and hope overflowing: God cares about the details of our lives. He cares about these children and that we have chosen to bring them into the world. He goes to supernatural lengths to reveal his love for us. Yes, there is heartache. Yes there is suffering. Yes, this world is far from perfect. But my goal is to live a life that looks for his hand and sees him at work. To see his tenderness in every miraculous detail. To see life as a sacred gift. To walk in faith. And to attest to the truth that when we walk in faith, we will walk in miracles.

THE MEMORY AND PROMISE OF LIGHT

There are moments, in the middle of the night, when the electricity of current events sends a shockwave through my sleeping body and wakes me, wide-eyed and shaken. What is going to happen to this broken world?

I see myself, gathering my children around me like the mother in a fairy tale, walking into a wood, thick with darkness. As we go deeper, the light seems to disappear and leaves us groping our way forward.

Dear children, we must press on through the darkness with an ever-kindled hope. There is a beautiful world on the other side.

Hope is not blind. Even in the deepest of darks, it discerns the next step. When there is no step illuminated, *hope sees by the mere memory of light.* We look back to remember God's faithfulness, and in this turning backward, we are moving forward by the sight of faith.

The promises of God are luminescent. They lie, hidden, scattered through every shadowed forest and are activated by the Word read, spoken, believed.

The wood is not the only world. And though we may find ourselves lost and uncertain, and at times afraid of the dark, hope and promise will light the way to lead us safely home.

THE DREAMS OF A STRANGER
NOVEMBER 2020

On November 22, I got a random message from someone I barely knew. *Hi!! Weird question. . . are you home?*

I thought it was odd, but odd things often happen to me, and I said, "Haha. Yes, what's up?"

The next text came. *Wondering if I could stop by real quick? I know. . .so random. . . Just trusting the Holy Spirit nudge. I would only stay 2 min. . .*

It was dark.

"Sure," I said.

See you in 10.

Heather knocked on my door, I answered it, and she smiled a beautiful humble smile, stepped over the threshold, and said these words to me:

"Hey Mackenzie. I know you are going to think I'm crazy (big, brave pause. . .), but can I see your basement? (Another pause.) Do you *have* a basement?"

And this was the beginning of the conversation that has changed my life. The beginning of the story of a miracle.

Randy and I first stepped over the same threshold, into this house, 14 years earlier. It looked different then. It was a brand-new, 2 bedroom, 2 bathroom house. At the time, I didn't think in terms of square footage, because my world was wide and still expanding, but this house was 1400 square feet of glorious space, and it was all ours. I knew I belonged there, moving through the yellow kitchen with the slant of late afternoon sun hitting the table. And in our deep red study in the wide corner of our bedroom, shelved with our favorite books, where we drank tea in the afternoons. We felt extravagant owning it because it was new and beautiful, full of character and walking distance to a small, historic town where we felt at home. We jokingly referred to it as The Chester Mansion when we had parties or get-togethers. It was clean. And quiet. And calm. And there was plenty of room to grow.

We spent our days working jobs, writing songs, and playing shows on weekends.

The following winter we had our first child. Our sweet Rosie, who changed our lives forever. We moved her to the corner of our upstairs bedroom and became a family.

A family that grew. A year and a half later, we had another baby. Paloma. Then came Kells, followed by Remy, followed by Heidi. Here I will pause.

Seven years later, our house felt increasingly smaller. By this time, we had moved our bedroom downstairs, and all five of our children shared the upstairs room. I felt claustrophobic in my own home. We taught music lessons several days a week in our living room, which meant that our children had to be quietly squeezed into one room for hours at a time, only coming out in 30 minute intervals if completely and absolutely necessary. We had people over in shifts all afternoon. While Randy taught guitar, I would sometimes visit with the mother of a student in my small and overly-crowded bedroom. In my memory, I see a bed, a couch, a tv, bookshelves, baskets of laundry, every surface piled high with papers and books, buckets of blocks and cars and trains overturned on the floor. And the thought of square footage became a reality to me. Because we had so little. And I longed for more.

This is when I began praying about our house. I did not see how we could fit another child into the dream-home we bought when we were young and the world was expanding, back when we were carrying a vision for our future that somehow didn't include living in this house with a family. I was too overwhelmed to consider selling our house, because that would mean every room would have to be clean at the same time. Which seemed just as impossible as time travel or moving Mount Everest or sleeping through the night.

Life had changed for us. We were playing fewer shows, settling more into family life, still trying to share our stories and our songs. I traded coffee shops where I loved to think and write for the corner of our living room. This is where I started my blog and where Randy began recording our songs. The same living room became the intimate venue where we shared our music. We recorded live videos from the couch after our kids went to sleep, and our home became the stage from which we shared our stories.

There was a long moment where we felt too overwhelmed to have more children. We prayed desperately for a clear answer to the question: should we be done? I felt maxed out on sleeplessness, on discipline, on space, on thought, on energy, on patience. I made the iconic pros and cons list, hoping to shed some light on the best course of action. The pros for being done stretched to the very bottom of the page. The cons were two things: 1)I wasn't sure if it pleased God for us to make that decision at this point. 2)I had a name for a boy that was not yet born.

And so I picked up the phone on a Friday and made the most impractical decision of my life. I canceled my Monday appointment to have my tubes tied. And I said yes to the idea of more children.

And I knew that it was faith. And this is where the miracles began.

When I learned I was pregnant with Azalea, I knew I was at the end of my own resources. We were not in crisis, but the amount of energy required to constantly dream up how we could make life work as a family of seven in a 2-bedroom house was exhausting. We worked from home, we homeschooled, we ate three meals a day all together every single day at the kitchen table. We recorded music, we made prolific creative messes, we had people in and out almost every day of the week for music lessons. I felt trapped in this house, but because of an economic shift in the housing market, selling was not an option. When I turned to God in prayer, it was in desperation.

A couple of months before the baby was going to be born, a friend called and told me that she wanted to enclose a large segment of our front porch to make a music room, where we could teach lessons without having our students enter the main part of our house. She gifted it to us at a great personal cost. Her sister was an architect with the eye of an artist, and we watched as the transformation happened before our eyes. It was a race to finish before the baby came. And it was finished just in time. A room that was not only functional, but extremely beautiful. Built with love and skill and attention to detail, walled with wood that had history. Randy and I began teaching music lessons in that wonderful space. Our children were free to spend the afternoons in any part of the house their hearts desired. If we had friends over, they could play in the living room. We could have tea in the kitchen. When we weren't teaching, we put a small portable bed in the new space, and our little Azalea Jane slept in the music room, adjacent to our own, for the first year and a half of her life.

Despite the beautiful addition, in January of 2018 I woke up and knew it was time for us to move. I couldn't see the layout of our house ever working for a family of our size. I began to clean one room at a time and photograph it. I filled journal after journal with prayers for a new house, the right house, a house where I wasn't spending one-third of my life trying to make it work. . . We decided to turn the large upstairs bedroom into two to add value to the house. We split the room and cut open a wall to make a closet, and to our surprise found an 8 x 12 foot attic space. This surprise was a small miracle of its own, and the closet became the munchkin bedroom of Heidi and Azalea. All prospects for selling and buying fell through. Closed door after closed door. I finally felt that I needed to rest my restlessness and trust that if God wanted to give us another house, He would give it to us without me throwing my life into the Zillow vortex. I began to settle back into the home he had given us and be grateful for the changes that we had made. We thought we were making them to sell our house, but it turned out we were making them to make our lives better here. We had somehow turned our two large bedrooms into, for all practical purposes, four. It made life easier for a season.

I still had a name for a baby in my heart. And on the page of my journal, I gathered my courage and made a definite decision that I would not refuse to open myself up to the possibility of having the child that I knew was one day coming, just because we didn't have a big enough house. Another leap of faith. Another season of prayer.

I miscarried the same year. My Daddy had helped me plant a beautiful garden early that spring. I will never forget how the marigolds and mint in the May-showers ministered to me from the window of our music room. How our house held me in my secret sadness, how I gained strength there, how my family gathered around me in those walls and brought me back to the beauty of life.

And then came Rune. When I found out he was a boy, I knew that I would finally see the face of the baby that had given me courage to walk in faith. My heart turned back to the house. I made lists, I brainstormed, I prayed for a vision, and for God to intervene. And I got an idea. I sent a text to the father of one of my piano students—a man who had a concrete business—and asked if he would be interested in bartering lessons for pouring a floor in our dank and musty, dirt-floor basement. To my astonishment, he said yes. And so we began the process that I never thought would be possible—creating a basement that we could use as part of our living space. We prayed and asked on facebook if any electricians or builders would be interested in bartering music lessons for labor. God brought both to us, and so on the most meager budget you can imagine, our house became bigger than we ever dreamed it could be. When I was in labor with Rune, our builder-friend was finishing the staircase that connected our house with the space below. It was a miracle. And I knew that God had heard my prayers and that he was pleased to give us this child and to provide for his needs.

Yes, the floor was concrete, and it was cold in the winter, and there was naked insulation in the walls and ceiling, but it was usable space with a hope for a future. Randy put a shop in, he walled up a utility closet which later became my office. In this space, I created a journaling course, wrote dozens of blog posts, and began a podcast in 2020.

And I felt the pleasure and presence of God in all of these changes, great and small.

When we found out we were expecting our eighth child, I knew our next need was more bedroom space. A light bulb went off when I thought of the shop room in the basement. How it could be perfect for Rosie and Paloma. I started making plans, but quickly learned that by no stretch of the imagination would we ever have the funds to buy a storage building that could be Randy's shop, and heat the basement, and add a drop ceiling in that room, and just in general make it feel like a room that wasn't a dungeon for them to sleep in. My heart went out to these sweet girls, ages 13 and 11, who help me so much with my life. I knew they had felt squeezed in our home just as I have, as child by child, they have selflessly given up more and more of their space and privacy. What I had dreamed was possible for them was a shut door. I began to pray that God would intervene.

I knew I couldn't spend any more time looking for houses. I had seen everything. And the last thing I wanted was a bigger house and more debt. It was depressing and overwhelming, and more than that, it was a huge waste of my precious time. I knew that the only way to make our space bigger was to get rid of stuff. So that is what I started doing. With a passion and fury that only a nesting mama can muster, I began getting rid of everything I didn't like, everything that I thought I might fix one day, everything that I thought was a great buy but never used. Clothes, books, kitchen gadgets, dishes, toys. . . Anything and everything. I went through every room of my house. I took vans full of stuff to the thrift store, feeling lighter with every load gone. I was on a rampage. People had to hide their stuff.

In my heart, I knew that God was going to either give us a lead on a new house or help us to come up with some creative solution to how we could add another child to this one. Because I was truly at the end of all my own resources, ideas, and energy where making it all work was concerned. I felt that I was waiting on a miracle, because there was nothing else I could do. And getting rid of stuff was a small act of obedience and faith, trusting that I was getting ready for whatever God had in mind.

And then it happened. About six weeks into the great purge, I got the text. Heather showed up on my doorstep. Late at night. With a beautiful humble smile and eyes twinkling as bright as stars.

"Can I see your basement? Do you *have* a basement?"

It turns out that this beautiful soul, who barely knew me, had been having *dreams* about my basement. Literal, sleeping dreams. Knowing nothing about my years of prayers, page after page in my journal where I had poured out my heart to God for more space for our children, for a way to make this house work, for an answer to whether we should go or stay. . . All she knew was a nudge from the Holy Spirit, bringing me to her mind over and over again. And *dreams* about my unremarkable unfinished basement.

It turns out that Heather runs a non-profit organization called The Everyday Good*, where she has begun a movement of everyday people seeing the needs around them and reaching out to change lives for the better. And standing in my living room, before ever walking down into my cold, dark basement, she leaned in like a lifelong friend and half-whispered that she believed The Everyday Good was supposed to do some work in our basement and asked me if that would be okay.

In that moment, every prayer I ever prayed flashed before my eyes. I stood on the threshold of my house of miracles, humbled and in awe. Through tears, I nodded, knowing I had been seen and heard by God. That He cares about these children we were bringing into the world. That He is able to answer our prayers in ways that we can not fathom. Our earthly resources are nothing compared with his riches. *He can access the dreams of strangers.* He can bring hearts and hands together for the common good of others. He can give a visionary woman the faith to rally a group of people who can grab hold of my mountain and cast it into the sea. Nothing is impossible with God.

Two months after this conversation, we packed up our suitcases and moved into a cabin for three weeks. We had no idea what we would come home to find, but we knew God was working out all of the details.

We didn't know about all the people who had joined together to meet our needs. We came home to a party with balloons and cupcakes and 900 square feet of beautiful, inspiring, warm, inviting, colorful, wonderful space. Through tears, I saw a houseful of people who had served our family. They put in a kitchenette and a bathroom and built a bedroom for our oldest daughters. They put in a heating system and finished all the walls and floors and ceilings, with a beautiful color palette and attention to detail. It was like looking at a picture in a magazine. But with all of our books and treasures in it. A place I wanted to be. The house was deep-cleaned almost beyond recognition, and there was new furniture in all the living spaces, as well as brand new mattresses on every bed. Every child had something special in his/her room. Every child saw the incredible, lavish love of God.

We learned later that over 60 volunteers had been in our home, selflessly giving their time, money, and support to our family. Most of whom we had never met. Words on paper cannot describe the palpable love of God that lingered in every room of our house when the job was done.

This is the work of the Kingdom. This is the kindness of our God. He is the God who sees our hearts and hears our prayers and is able to do more than we could ever think or imagine.

He cares about the secret details of our lives. And He is able and willing to work miracles.

After the crowd said goodbye, and our family was left, looking around in awe and wonder at the home that had just been given to us, Paloma, then 11 years old, looked up at me with wide, grateful eyes, and said, "Mom, this is like the best dream ever."

There wasn't a better way to describe it.

Sometimes the answer to our prayers begin in the most obscure and unexpected places. In the story my family will tell for the rest of our lives, the deepest dreams of our heart were known by God. He told our secrets to someone who could do what we could not. And he spoke and worked miracles through the dreams of a stranger.

*For more on The Everyday Good, visit https://www.theeverydaygood.com/

ONE SMALL GARDEN

Tending the Life I Am Given
March 18, 2021

How do I keep finding myself here in the middle of the night?
I should be sleeping. I tossed and turned an hour before
surrendering to the river-rush of words that swept me up in
its current and lifted my body out of bed and onto the quiet
bank of the 3 a.m. kitchen table. During the day, the needs
overtake me. I take them one by one. This blessed house,
these beautiful children, the book I am always writing in my
head. The garden we are planning. Three meals a day, the
shaping of souls, the lighting of fires, the putting them out. . .
The thought of the baby who is coming in a few short weeks
and how he will sweetly upend our lives again. Thoughts of
my mother, who would have understood. I draw strength
from the memory of her completed life while grieving deeply
that she is not here to walk through this birth with me.

Life is so complex. One minute you are planning out your
garden—seed packets sprawled all across the table,
handwritten lists and little diagrams everywhere. . . You are
imagining the seed going into the ground and the eventual
harvest. You can almost taste the ripe red tomato, flavored by
the full sun. You see yourself basking in the uncomplicated
joy, tasting the fruit of your labor.

And the next minute you see your children before you, all rising up out of the ground, reaching for full maturation. All needing varying degrees of shade and sun and thirsty for water. You see the weeds creeping up around them. You wonder if you prepared the soil properly. If the roots went down deep enough. You are aware of your short-comings as a gardener and that each season you are learning from the mistakes of seasons past. You know there are torrential rains ahead and droughts and pests that you have yet to learn by name. And yet, you have that shining hope of the fruit of their lives. That God will grant you the grace to partner with him in the good work of the garden. And that He will cause these beautiful young plants to grow strong and endure.

I am set upon this earth to tend the life I was given. It is one small life. One garden. I hope I am doing this right. There are some things I put in the soil that never came up. But there are seeds I tossed, almost casually, over my shoulder that have taken root and grown into trees, full of fruit.

Oh God, by your grace and mercy, I ask that you teach me to tend my garden. Make it a place where people can stop and sit and see your beauty in every changing season. Where there is color and fragrance and the quivering beauty of blossoming trees. Where birds sing and life is everywhere and everlasting. I want to be so much more than a bare plot of earth. Work me, Lord. And cause beautiful things to grow from my life.

Vision and Hindsight
A Tale of Two Lists
January 28, 2020

The year flew by. This morning I was sitting at the kitchen table, lamenting all the things that I meant to do last year—my open journal with the list I scribbled down, wide-eyed, like a child on her birthday, a January ago. Beautiful vision. And just like that, I blinked, and those twelve months are memories, rising up like balloons and disappearing into the sky.

So many things didn't happen. So many goals not met. So many days where we were stuck in a holding pattern of one sort or another. . . The third trimester of pregnancy, birth, life with a newborn, walking the pace of the smallest child, doing each day and then doing the next.

Last January, I had not yet noticed the heavy shadow of grief looming over my life. I didn't know that I would be losing the radiant warmth and beauty of my mother's presence. Her life set like a brilliant sun, and the light of all of my days are now colored by the shadow of her passing.

I wanted to do everything. I wanted to do everything right. I wanted that list to be checked off and graded as easily as my elementary spelling tests. A+ parenting. I did it all.

But the reality is, as hard as I tried, my vision for the year was not big enough to encompass the reality of what God was working out in our lives. I delivered a beautiful baby boy. I lost my mother. Both of these experiences, on opposite ends of the life-spectrum, have flooded my days with unexpected light and shadow. Both experiences have slowed my pace and caused me to pause, look out the window at the rain falling, and rethink what life is all about.

Look outside. The rain is bitterly cold. This winter has been long. There is so little green. The trees look as though they could never recover the color and warmth of springtimes past. So many clouds. So much of the world in shadow.

But there are secrets under the soil. The beautiful life of every green thing lies safely dormant, protected from the biting January cold.

I am so blessed with the joy of a newborn's daily presence. My darling boy, experiencing everything for the first time. . . His dear little face wakes me up to wonder. His pure and sweet true love for me. His tiny, careful, gentle touch. His perfectly turned-up nose. There is just nothing like a baby. And his little life, which God, in his lovingkindness, gave me as a beautiful gift between the hollow ache of losing a baby in the womb and the ocean waves of sadness following my mother's death, means more to me than I could ever say. This little life is pure sunshine. And in the shadow of a season of great loss, I am more thankful than ever for the brilliant light behind a baby's eyes. It will make so many good things grow.

I am humbled by the great work that God is doing in my life in allowing me to be a mother of seven children. Sometimes it is hard to know if the seeds you are planting are going to take root and grow. The work is so long and slow. And there is no guarantee against bitter winters and false springs. And I am not much of a gardener by nature. But I am trying to learn. Season by season.

I closed my journal and began to pray.

God, I offer myself to you. Use me. You know I am not getting it all right. Use me in spite of my inability to figure it all out. Use me as I stumble through grief and blunder my way through parenting. Use me as I fumble my way through homeschooling, as I start and restart every kind of daily routine imaginable trying to make life work in each new season. You know my heart. I know I am never going to get it all right. But I know there is even grace for my mistakes and weaknesses. I just need vision for this day. And that is something you promise to those who are seeking you. That you will be the voice saying, "This is the way. Walk in it." Use me, God. Use what is fragrant and in bloom, use what is dormant for a day in the future, use what once was but no longer bears fruit and throw it into the compost heap of my life.

Amen.

I turned to a new page of a new journal. I started a new list. Of things that actually happened last year. All the big things I could remember. And I began to feel my heavy heart lifting. Like helium.

We had a baby. We took a trip to the beach. We added a basement of 900 square feet of usable creative space to our home. I got a wheel and we began learning to make pottery. We started epic board game nights with the kids. My young sons picked up new instruments and began playing at church. My girls learned to decorate cakes. We wrote songs and stories, created art, read stacks of books, filled notebooks with our own unique hands and voices. We added instruments to the family collection and accumulated hundreds of hours of family practice. We built a fire pit and camped in a tent. The kids learned to ride bikes. They learned to use the computer to create songs and movies and comics. I wrote more and from places deep in my heart that continue to open up and surprise me. I inherited my beautiful mother's watercolors and brushes. We baptized four children. We met around the table three times a day for nearly 365 days to share a meal and talk and be together. So much fruit. So much growth. So much we learned.

The year flew by. I had almost forgotten how much time we spent working in the family garden. This morning I drank a cup of coffee, scribbled down a list of all the wonderful things we accomplished over the last twelve months. Beautiful hindsight. My heart was light like a birthday balloon. And I walked into the morning ready to celebrate this beautiful life. It is such a gift. It is such a mystery. And I am reminded that as I pray for vision and grace and daily do the best that I can, I will continue to see beautiful things growing out of this rich, fertile soil in every season to come.

BEAUTY IN THE MIDST OF DARKNESS

APRIL 23, 2021

There is so much darkness in this world. It presses in against us. In the middle of the night, it enters into our minds in the quiet spaces and works to leave a shadow that lingers even when the morning comes. We wake to light, but its brilliance is dimmed by the memory of those dark thoughts.

I was overwhelmed by something I saw when I was trying to take a sane look at what is happening in the world. My heart sank. *This* is the world I live in. *This* is the world where we must raise our children. *This* is the only option for worlds into which I can bring this baby, due today. He is just leaving the tender hands of God, who knit him together in my womb, and I prepare to welcome him into only *this* world. . . How will these precious children learn to see when they are surrounded by so much darkness? How will their roots grow strong and their lives flourish in a world that is cast in so much shadow and has so little sunlight?

I gathered up my little boy for a nap and sang to him. I inhaled deeply the sweetness of his voice. I watched his eyes softly dim and fall into perfect, trusting sleep. I slept with him in my arms. Dreamless.

I woke, my heart still heavy. I walked into the kitchen, pulled out my journal, made myself a cup of tea, and turned on music. Voices singing. Words of peace. Music bursting forth into the silence and filling every space with its unrelenting hope and beauty. And in a moment, my heart was lifted. My darkness was lightened. The beauty of music. The power of words. The souls of people who speak life over the death and decay that is all around us. The atmosphere was completely changed.

This is not the only world. Truly, the world we see is just a shadow of the real and invisible kingdom of God. We belong to a world where there is light and life everlasting. Where hope outshines every fear. Where faith is given substance. Where miracles happen. Where our lives have meaning and purpose. Where our children can grow into the people that God has created them to be. And even in the world where we now use our five senses, we catch glimpses into that other world. Through beauty.

Oh my soul, the tender love of God shines forth in the shimmering petals of the pale-purple irises. In the leaf-buds that whisper promises of future flowers. In the seed that springs up from the barren earth. The gentle rains, the song of birds, the hum of life that makes all the earth sweetly tremble.

The love of God is wrapped up in tiny packages of words: peace, trust, rest, light, hope, love, mercy. . . I open them up as I need them. I pour them into cups of tea and drink them down medicinally. I infuse them into music and breathe them into my lungs.

My heart continues to beat. And while there is life, there is light. There is so much beauty to be seen and experienced and shared. I search for it. I gather the seeds of it. I plant it, I water it, I tend to it. And I harvest it. And I make it my life's work to bring the abundance of beauty to the table and share.

THE WOMAN AND THE SEED
(A PARABLE)

This is a true story. It is the story of a woman who fell in love with a man. She married him with a certain picture of what life would be like in the back of her mind. It looked like a garden in springtime. Everything beautiful was in bloom. Every bird was singing.

They were happy. They were making life work, braiding their lives in a chord that would never be untied. Between the demands of daily life, they were together as much as life allowed, and they were working toward a common purpose. They were trying to cultivate a quiet seed of meaning.

They thought they were planting one kind of seed. They thought it was a fig tree. They dropped it in the ground where fig trees grow best—with full sun and sheltered from the chill of the north wind. They imagined themselves a few years down the road, picnicking in its shade, eating homemade bread and fig preserves.

But it wasn't a fig tree. It took them a couple of years to figure this out. Because neither of them had much experience in tending to a garden. Together, they looked at the small tree that was growing out of the ground. They scratched their heads, laughed at their naivety, and gave a little sigh about how figs were good but there were other fruits just as delicious. And wouldn't it be a surprise to see what was going to grow there...

The woman and the man spent the next several years watering, adding compost, and checking the lifesigns of the little tree in each season. When they had time, they would scour the libraries for tree identification guides. They brought home armfuls of books. They looked on every page. They found similarities, but were never able to find an exact match for what was growing in their own backyard. They tried to piece together a way to nurture this little tree, which, despite their limited understanding of how to care for it, continued to grow taller and more robust day by day.

Meanwhile, there was normal life to be reckoned with. The day-to-dayness of life. Weathering storms and enjoying full days of sunshine. It became a different kind of picture. Not a garden in full bloom. But a garden in every season. The long-dayed yellow gold of summer, leaves of crimson and the cool-crisp autumn air, winter's still and bitter cold, and back again to the rain and sweet green of spring.

And through every season, year after year, storm and sun after sun and storm, this little seed of meaning continued to grow into something that both puzzled and surprised the man and the woman. They could never exactly name it. They could never find a picture in a book and say, "Here it is. This is how we are supposed to feed and water it. These are the best conditions for this tree to grow. It will produce fruit if we do this. . ." Instead, they continued to watch for signs of flourishing. They tended to it in drought and in flood. It grew. It grew. It grew. It grew bigger and taller than any other tree in the garden. It became a home for a myriad of birds and small creatures. It became a shade from the scorching summer heat. The man and woman would sometimes put out a blanket and sit under the tree. They would laugh that they once thought this was a fig tree, as it had now grown taller than any fig tree they had ever seen.

"But will it ever produce fruit?" The woman asked.

With a trembling hope in her soul, she heard a still and quiet yes. This tree was different than any they had ever seen. They expected one thing but grew another. And here it was, towering above them, something bigger and grander than they had ever imagined growing up out of their own backyard. It was alive and healthy. And it was growing, surviving, and thriving even amidst the natural disasters of life.

It was years. Years. Years. Years. Long years.

The man and woman grew older.

One day, the woman looked up and saw flowers. The flowers became fruit. The fruit was unlike any she had ever tasted. It didn't have a name. But it was ripened to perfection. It was delicious. It was medicinal. It produced a handful of seeds which she scattered in the side yard. She made jam. She made tea. She and her husband sat in the backyard and enjoyed the fruit of the seed that they planted so many years ago.

The scattered seeds were carried by birds and wind. Many of them grew to produce fruit of their own, which in turn produced more trees which produced more fruit and so on and so on.

This story eventually comes to a close. But not in the lifetime of the man and the woman. They died long before they saw the orchards growing just down the road from where that first seed was planted.

They were forgotten. But together, they planted a seed, which grew into a tree, which grew into an orchard which continues to bear fruit.

The Parable Explained:

This story may be about you. It is also about me.

I am the woman. The labor of my life is the tree. I can only see the ending by faith, because even now, I am looking for fruit.

I used to think my life was about something else. Always the Kingdom of Heaven. Always for the glory of Christ. These were my deepest hopes—that my life would reflect his love and light. But I thought those themes would play themselves out differently. I thought it would be a bigger and bolder statement.

I have come to see that in this season of my life, being a mother is my calling. I say this humbly, because God knows that I have wrestled with a surrender of my own will and desires. I have asked God many times to give me grace to walk this calling out because, in all honesty, I feel unqualified. Every child is so different and comes with such a unique set of instructions for care. They are all written in code. And you have to figure each one out as you go. Truly, raising our children is like watching that tree come up from the ground. Scratching our heads, wondering how in the world we ended up with this kind of life when we were so sure we were planting something else. But here we are with this grand and glorious tree, one of its kind. Beautiful, full of life and wonder, and yet there is always the question of the future fruit. Will this tree withstand all the natural disasters of life? Will these little ones grow up to be who they are meant to be?

I confess that I have sometimes thought of these years of giving birth and tending to the constant needs of young children as a season to pass through in order to get back to the real purpose of my life. It can feel like so little is actually being accomplished. I have wanted to "get on with my life." God has gently and lovingly spoken to my spirit time and again, "*This* is your life." Nothing has changed me more than the heart-and-soul surrender to the simple and wildly profound call of motherhood. I am humbled by his love and grace which has brought me here. I am finding new identity in Christ as I step into the role which he has set before me. I am humbled by the gentle wisdom and inexhaustible love of children. I am in awe of the life I have been given.

I am finding deep meaning within the walls of this house. We are raising a family. It isn't the fig tree I imagined. But it is becoming something that only God could have brought forth from my life. A tree that only he can sustain and teach me how to water, how to protect in storm and drought, a tree that only he, at the right moment, can speak into flowering. It requires faith to look ahead and see where this is going. It isn't just about this tree. This little family. But it is about the fruit of a life that is openly turned to God, a life that can bring forth the seed he is planting—whatever it looks like—and can water it and nurture it to fruition. When we turn our lives to Christ and willingly offer ourselves to cultivate the seed of meaning that he has planted in our hearts, the work of our lives becomes more than the tree we are planting. It becomes something that we, in our lifetime, may only begin to see. It becomes the full fruit of an orchard. Because a life that is surrendered to God will always yield exponential fruit.

This is my story. The story of a woman who, along with her husband, planted a seed, which one day became a tree, which will one day, by faith and through the grace and covenant of God, become an orchard full of good, sweet fruit.

THE END

ACKNOWLEDGMENTS

I've been dreaming of this moment for so many years: My book is written. The process has been a long and tedious one, and there have been many times I've been tempted to quit for sheer lack of courage. Writing a book, like other daunting creative ambitions, can feel lonely and burdensome at times. I'm grateful I have not had to write my story alone.

I feel confident the book you are holding in your hands would not exist without the faithful and generous support of my Patrons. There is no way I could have allowed myself to devote the long hours to this work without it. To everyone who has joined my Patreon, even for a short season, thank you from the bottom of my heart. You have given me the permission, resources, and courage I needed to see this project through. I hope you like the book.

To Victoria, who was there all along the way, speaking life into each step of the process, believing in my work and cheering me on. Thank you, dear friend.

To Nance, who was the first supporter of my writing. You have removed so many obstacles from my life. And you have made so many things possible that were only desperate prayers and fervent hopes. Thank you. I love you.

To Heather and The Everyday Good, it has been two years, and I still have no words. Thank you for the beautiful, glorious, inspiring space. And for giving me and my children a memory of God's tangible love and faithfulness that we will never forget.

To Michelle, for lending me your houses when I needed a quiet space. And for always talking me down off the ledge when I wanted to quit. Not just the book, but putting my voice out there. I am so thankful for your friendship.

To Dea, for knowing just what to say when I needed to hear it and for pointing me in the direction of writing and finishing this book. And for loving me like I'm your own.

To Melanie, for always believing in me, and for routinely having pizzas delivered to my house, which freed up time for me to write and made lunch a party.

To Tanya, GinaMarie, Rachel, Dea, Melanie, and Jessica for being my first readers and giving your valuable feedback.

To Adrienne, for inspiring me and encouraging me, even from afar, for all these years. Your lifelong friendship is a treasure to me.

To Crystal, for your artist's eye and your constant encouragement. Thank you for celebrating this with me, week by week.

Susan, thank you for the prayers you have prayed over my life and for all the seeds you have sown into it. You have given me hope and courage at so many critical moments. I love you.

To my highschool English teacher, Marcia Martin, who taught me how to choose the right word. When I was a teenager, I used to imagine writing a book and thanking you in the acknowledgements. Now I have done it.

To the memory of Leroy Young, who taught me the basics of drawing, photography, and graphic design and told me I was an artist.

To all the friends who read and subscribe to my substack, and especially those who have pledged their support. Thank you from the bottom of my heart.

And to all of my readers and friends who listen to The Sacred Everyday Podcast, thank you for allowing me to be a part of your lives. It is both humbling and inspiring to know you are there.

To my husband, Randy. Thank you for understanding that desperate look in my eyes and giving me time to write this book. Also for bringing the comic relief to my life and making me laugh till I cry on a regular basis. Thank you for your faith, which I have borrowed over and over again. And for being willing to share this life with me. I love and admire you.

To Rosie, Paloma, Kells, Remy, Heidi, Azalea, Rune, and Haven. Thank you for bringing so much joy and beauty to my world and for all the ways you teach and inspire me. You are my greatest treasures. Your mama loves you.

Oh, God, thank you so much that this book is done. I pray you will use it for your glory. Please continue to teach me how to see you in each moment of this sacred everyday life. Amen.

Connect with Mackenzie

Blog: www.mackenziechester.com

Podcast: The Sacred Everyday

Instagram: @thesacredeveryday

Facebook: Mackenzie Chester

Substack: https://mackenziechester.substack.com

Patreon: https://www.patreon.com/mackenziechester

Email: hi@mackenziechester.com

Made in the USA
Columbia, SC
05 January 2025

51303619R00143